NO NO NO NO NO NO NO NO NO
NO NO NO NO NO NO NO NO NO NO
NO NO NO NO NO NO NO NO NO
NO NO NO NO NO NO NO NO NO
NO NO NO NO NO NO NO NO NO NO
NO NO NO NO NO NO NO NO NO
NO NO NO NO NO NO NO NO
NO NO NO NO NO NO NO
NO NO NO NO NO NO
NO NO
NO
NO

# REJECTION PROOF

# PROOF

## How to Beat **Fear** and Become **Invincible**

### JIA JIANG

rh

BOOKS

Published by Random House Books in 2016

1 3 5 7 9 10 8 6 4 2

Random House Books
20 Vauxhall Bridge Road
London SW1V 2SA

Random House Books is part of the
Penguin Random House group of companies whose
addresses can be found at global.penguinrandomhouse.com

Penguin
Random House
UK

First published in the United States in 2015 by Harmony Books,
an imprint of the Crown Publishing Group, a division
of Penguin Random House LLC, New York

First published in Great Britain by Random House Books in 2015

www.randomhouse.co.uk

A CIP catalogue record for this book is available from the British Library

ISBN 9781847941459

Printed and bound in Great Britain by Clays Ltd, St Ives plc

Penguin Random House is committed to a sustainable future
for our business, our readers and our planet. This book is made
from Forest Stewardship Council® certified paper

MIX
Paper from
responsible sources
FSC
www.fsc.org   FSC® C018179

# PROOF

Jia Jiang is founder of the popular blog and video series '100 Days of Rejection'. His story has been covered by dozens of news outlets, including *Bloomberg Businessweek*, Yahoo! News, the Huffington Post, *Forbes*, Inc.com, MTV, Gawker, the *Daily Mail*, Fox News and CBS's *The Jeff Probst Show*. A native of Beijing, China, Jiang came to the United States as a teenager to pursue his dream of becoming an entrepreneur. Jiang holds an MBA from Duke University and a bachelor's degree in computer science from Brigham Young University.

## Praise for *Rejection Proof*

'[An] entertaining study of rejection in all its many manifestations.'
*Daily Mail*

'Jia's compelling and inspiring book is a wonderful example of how shifting our perspective can allow us to really see what makes us tick.'
Dan Ariely, author of *Predictably Irrational*

'I hope you buy two copies of this book because as soon as you read it, you'll want to give it to someone else who needs a boost of bravery too.'
Jon Acuff, author of *Do Over* and *Start*

'*Rejection Proof* is a fun, thoughtful examination of how to overcome our fears and dare to live more boldly. You have no idea what you can achieve until you try!'

Nancy Duarte, author of *Slide:ology*

'A clever and inspiring read that will change the way you approach anything that may seem out of reach. This book made me want to look fear in the eye . . . and then kick it in the ass.' Alison Levine, author of *On the Edge*

To Grandma:

as a lifelong teacher, you taught me something that's more
valuable than anything I've learned in school: being a good person.

I miss you so much.


And


To Uncle Brian:

thank you for being my second father in my life.

Your support and mentorship mean the world to me.

# CONTENTS

# REJECTION
## PROOF

# PROLOGUE

**N**OVEMBER 18, 2012. IT WAS AN UNUSUALLY HOT AFTER-noon in Austin, Texas—but that's not why I was sweating. I was driving my dusty RAV4 slowly through a random middle-class suburb in the northwest part of town, looking for a door to knock on. I'd already passed hundreds of front doors, willing myself to pick one. But given what I was about to do, every house looked terrifying.

"OK, stop being a coward," I muttered to myself, parking in front of a one-story, redbrick house with a nice garden. Poking out of the flower bed was a small, decorative cross. I hoped the cross signaled that a peaceful, churchgoing family lived there, not a KKK member. Either way, I hoped they wouldn't turn violent on a Sunday afternoon.

As I got out of the car, I wondered whether anyone was

peering through their drapes at the unexpected sight before them: a grown man wearing shin guards and cleats, holding a soccer ball in one hand and video-recording himself with an iPhone held in the other. "Well, this one is a little bit risky," I said to my phone. "I am going to ask someone to open up their backyard for me to play soccer in it. We'll see what happens."

As I walked toward the door, I could feel my heart pounding. My cleats crunched through piles of dead leaves, and crows cawed from their perches in nearby trees. It felt ominous, like the beginning of a scary movie. That walkway seemed like the longest in the world.

Finally at the door, I knocked gently, fearing I would convey the wrong intention by pounding too hard. There was no response. I knocked again, with a bit more force. Still no response. It was only then that I noticed the doorbell. I pressed it. A moment later, the door swung open.

Standing in front of me was a large man in his forties, wearing a gray T-shirt with a giant Texas flag on it. Coming from the living room behind him I could hear the voices of TV football announcers and the faint buzz of a cheering stadium crowd. His name was Scott, I later learned. Like many Texans, he was a rabid Dallas Cowboys fan, and my knock came just as the game between the Cowboys and the Cleveland Browns was heading into overtime.

"Hey there," I said in my best Texas drawl, gathering my courage. "Do you think it's possible for you to take a picture of me playing soccer in your backyard?"

The man's eyes narrowed for a second. Then he glanced downward at my cleats. "Playing soccer in my backyard," he repeated, slowly.

"It's . . . uh . . . for a special project," I said.

After what seemed like a minute, but was probably just seconds, the Cowboys fan looked me right in the eyes and gave me my answer. . . .

CHAPTER 1

# MEETING REJECTION

**Y**OU'RE PROBABLY WONDERING WHY I WAS STANDING at this man's front door and what I meant by "special project." Was this a new sales strategy I was practicing? A dare? A social experiment? Actually, it was a little bit of each. It was part of a one-hundred-day journey to overcome my fear of rejection—a journey that gave me a new perspective on business and humanity, and gave me tools to be better at almost everything. By challenging myself to seek out rejection again and again, I came to see rejection—and even the world around me—very differently. It changed my life—and I hope that by reading about my journey, it might change yours as well.

But before I tell you what happened next, maybe I should go back a bit—back to the start.

It was July 4, 2012, just after sunset. Thousands of people were gathered at our local community park, waiting for
the Independence Day fireworks to start. My wife, Tracy,
sat next to me on our blanket, rubbing her belly. She was
eight months pregnant with our first child. All around us,
kids were running with Frisbees and ice cream cones, families were unpacking picnic baskets, beer bottles clinked, and
laughter filled the air. Everyone seemed so happy, so filled
with summertime joy.

Everyone but me.

In many ways, I was living the American dream. At just
thirty years old, I had a secure six-figure job at a Fortune 500
company. Tracy and I owned a 3,700-square-foot house with
a pond view. We even had a golden retriever named Jumbo—
the quintessential suburban American dog—and now we
were weeks away from the birth of our son. Best of all, my
wife and I had an incredible relationship, and not a day went
by that I didn't realize how lucky I was to be loved by such an
amazing woman. In other words, I should have been over-
joyed with my circumstances. But the truth was, I was as depressed as I could be. My misery wasn't personal, though—it
was professional.

I grew up in Beijing, China, at a time when every school-
age child was taught to be a model worker and a building block for the growth of the nation. But being a model
worker—in China or anywhere—had never been my dream.
Instead, ever since I was little, I had fantasized about being an
entrepreneur. While other kids played sports or video games,
I devoured the biographies of Thomas Edison and Panasonic
founder Konosuke Matsushita, looking for clues about how

to become a great innovator. When I was fourteen, Bill Gates visited Beijing, his first-ever trip to my hometown. And I became obsessed with his story of founding Microsoft. I tore down all the sports memorabilia I had on my bedroom walls and made my fantasy about entrepreneurship a life goal. I vowed to become the next Bill Gates and invent an amazing technology product that would take the world by storm. I pestered my family into buying me a brand-new top-of-the-line computer and started teaching myself how to write programming code. I even wrote a letter to them (which I still have) promising that my company would be so successful that I would buy Microsoft by the time I was twenty-five. Drawn in by flashy Hollywood depictions of America and the fact that Bill Gates lived there, I also believed I would one day move to the United States to fulfill that destiny.

When I was sixteen, I was presented with an opportunity to become a high school exchange student in the United States and go to an American college afterward. I jumped on it. The transition was difficult, to say the least. The language and culture barriers were a struggle to overcome, and I was sad to leave my loving family. To make matters worse, the situation I walked into was not a good one. My first year in the United States was spent in rural Louisiana, of all places, and the exchange program did a lousy job background-checking my host family. As a result, my first "home away from home" was in the creepy house of a family of criminals. I learned that their older son had been convicted of murder a year prior to my arrival, and it was his bed that I slept in. Even worse, two days after my arrival, my host parents stole all my money.

Sleeping in the bed of a murderer and losing all my money

was not the introduction to America that I'd been expecting. I'd left the protective, supportive bubble of my own family in China only to land with a family that immediately broke my trust. It scared me, and I didn't know what to do. Ultimately, I reported their theft to my high school superintendent, who then reported it to the police. My host parents were arrested, and the mortified folks at the exchange program moved me to another home—luckily, the home of a wonderful family. There I not only reexperienced love and trust, gained spiritual faith, I also learned that there are good people and bad people in the world, and they would certainly not treat me the same way.

Throughout this shaky start, my dream of becoming an entrepreneur in America stayed as strong as ever. In fact, I didn't believe there was any way that I could fail. Becoming an entrepreneur felt more like my fate or destiny than any sort of choice on my part. The goal was so deeply embedded in my heart that I don't think I could have shaken it if I tried.

After one year in high school, and another six months at an English as a second language institute, my English had vastly improved. It was January 1999; I was ready for college. I still remember my first day at the University of Utah. I was just seventeen years old. There had been a snowstorm the night before, and the entire campus was covered in white. I can still hear the sounds my feet made—*voo, voo, voo*—as I walked through the snow to class that morning, leaving the first set of footprints of the day. The universe was a fresh snowfield in front of me, ready for me to blaze my own trail and become the next great immigrant entrepreneur in America. I had youth, hope, and energy on my side. Everything seemed possible.

My first real chance ~~to~~ launch my entrepreneurial dream came while I was still in college. For years, I'd constantly been thinking up cool new devices that I could invent. One day, as I was flipping through an old photo album, I saw a picture of myself roller-skating as a kid. Some of my happiest childhood memories were of roller-skating with my friends. Suddenly, I started thinking about how cool it would be to combine a tennis shoe with a Rollerblade. Kids and adults could be walking one moment and gliding around with their friends the next. The world would become a giant rink, and happiness would be widespread!

Excited, I pulled out my sketchbook and started drawing out various ideas for how to functionally embed wheels into a shoe. I loved the idea so much that I even drew a formal blueprint to submit with a future patent application. It took me an entire weekend. Afterward, I felt like I'd created the *Mona Lisa*.

Sure, it may not have been the most life-changing idea the world had ever seen. But it was *my* idea, and I thought it was awesome, and it could be the invention that launched my entrepreneurial career.

I have an uncle in San Diego—my father's younger brother—whom I've always held in extremely high regard. While my parents were both very easygoing, my uncle was very strict and demanding, which somehow made me want his approval even more. To be honest, I was scared of him as a child. But I always knew that he cared about me and wanted me to succeed. After I moved to the United States, he and I became even closer, and I viewed him almost as another father, so much so that I would later name my son after him. I always felt much surer of myself when he liked my ideas and my choices. So I sent him a copy of my drawings, excited to get his reaction to the "shoes with wheels" idea and hoping for encouragement.

Imagine my disappointment when instead of support I received a verbal smackdown. My uncle thought my idea was silly, and he chastised me for focusing on something so far-fetched when I should be concentrating on school and improving my English.

I felt so dispirited that I tossed my sketches into a drawer and never moved forward with the idea. If my own uncle had rejected my idea, I felt sure that the world would hate it even more—and I wanted no part of being rejected in public by strangers. Instead, I focused on getting good grades and continuing to improve my English. Using thousands of flash cards, I spent many hours every day learning and memorizing new English words. Excelling at school was a surefire way to win the approval of my family, especially my uncle. And I didn't just want their approval—I craved it. I told myself that straight As and an impressive vocabulary might also make me a better entrepreneur someday.

My good grades did pay off in some way. I landed a scholarship offer from Brigham Young University, where I transferred and completed college. Yet I felt like I'd missed something much bigger.

Two years later, a man named Roger Adams patented exactly the same idea (shoe-skates) and founded the company

Heelys. In 2007, just after its IPO, Heelys was valued at almost $1 billion. Meanwhile, my blueprint sat in a drawer, gathering dust. Sadly, it's not the only blueprint in there. Over the years, I've come up with dozens of new ideas that I thought had the potential to turn into successful products. But rather than pursuing them, I just added them to the pile—and then gently closed the drawer.

Of course, there's no guarantee that my shoe-skate innovation would have succeeded the same way that Adams's did—or that any of my other ideas would have become the foundation of a successful company. But I never even gave them—or myself—a chance to find out. I rejected my own ideas before they could be rejected by the world. Giving up at the first sign of rejection felt much safer than putting my ideas out there to be further criticized. It was so much easier to do the rejecting all by myself.

But every time I saw kids skating on Heelys in malls, sidewalks, and playgrounds, every time I read an article about Adams turning his childhood passion into a pop culture craze, I thought about what could have been. The pain and regret were unbearable.

I thought that I'd feel the freedom to become an entrepreneur after I graduated from college, with my computer science degree fresh in hand. But the opposite happened. The family and social pressures didn't fade away. If anything, they became stronger. Instead of winning others' approval by being a good student, I now wanted to win their admiration by having a strong and stable career. I hadn't started a company in college, and I didn't start one after college either. Instead, I tried out job after job until I realized that being a computer programmer wasn't my thing. Scared that I'd chosen the wrong path, I changed career tracks in a way that made me feel safe: I reentered the familiar comforts of school, this time pursuing an MBA at Duke University. Afterward, I took a marketing job at a Fortune 500 company. I thought the accolades and approval I would receive from my prestigious degree and my new six-figure income would satisfy my inner entrepreneur. I couldn't have been more wrong.

On the first day of my new job, my boss asked me write a short self-introduction. One of the questions was "What would you do if you weren't doing this?" Without hesitation, I wrote down "Being an entrepreneur." Someone then asked me: "Then why aren't you?" I didn't know how to answer it.

It's amazing how fast the years fly by—and how big the gap can grow between your vision for yourself and the reality of your life. Simply put, I'd sold out my dream. That teenager walking on snow hadn't become the next Bill Gates. Instead, he became a marketing manager sitting quietly on his cozy little rung of the corporate ladder, miserably collecting good income. Once in a while, the envy of friends or the pride of my family would give me temporary but false assurance that I was doing well in life. But for me, the relentless ticking clock of life was like the sun, melting away the snowfield of my dreams and ambition. I remember one day, after coming back from work, I locked myself in my closet, sobbing for hours. I hadn't cried for a long time.

Now, sitting on our July 4 blanket, I couldn't help feeling that my entrepreneurial dream was over before it ever took off. If I hadn't taken the leap to try building a start-up as an eighteen-year-old college student, or as a twenty-two-year-old single guy, or as a twenty-eight-year-old MBA, how could I do it as a thirty-year-old middle manager just weeks from becoming a father? Being a parent brought with it a whole new set of responsibilities that I thought would require me to put my dream permanently to rest.

A loud explosion went off in the sky, and the darkness was lit up with bright colors. Sitting there, contemplating my future, it was almost as if I could see in the sky an imaginary slide show of what the rest of my life would look like. At work, I'd continue to sell more products, train more employees, and establish more processes. At home, we'd have one or two more kids, sending them off to school and eventually to college. The slide show ended at my own funeral, with someone giving a touching but typical eulogy praising my loyalty and dependability. It was a eulogy for just another good guy—not the world-changing entrepreneur I had dreamed of becoming.

Tracy looked over at me. For weeks, she'd known that I was miserable, and she knew why. "You can have another car, house, promotion, or job. But you can't live with this kind of regret," she said. And then my wife—my very pregnant wife—did something amazing. She issued me a challenge. She told me to quit my job, take six months to start a company from scratch, and work as hard as I could to build it. If by the end of that time I still had no traction and no investment, I would hop back on the corporate ladder.

I felt a surge of adrenaline at the thought of truly being free to follow my dreams. But then fear quickly set in. If I failed, there would be no guarantee I could get a job nearly as good, and I would be seen as a fool in the eyes of my friends. And then there was the small matter of Tracy's parents.

Like me, Tracy was born in China, and her parents have very traditional ideas of what constitutes work and success. My father-in-law, like most fathers-in-law, was skeptical about the guy who had won his daughter's heart. But based on what Tracy told me, I learned that he liked how I provided for my family. Wouldn't quitting my job drive him over the edge? "I'll take care of my parents and their concerns," she said. "You just make sure you give everything you have—and leave no regret." There have been many moments in my life when I've realized that I married up. This was one of them.

For the longest time, I had fantasized about the day I would quit my job and start a company. Now that day had arrived— and I wasn't sure how to go about it. Should I pull a Jerry Maguire, making a loud speech in the office before storming out? Or should I do something even more dramatic, making a grand exit like the JetBlue flight attendant who quit by going down the evacuation slide of his plane?

I didn't do either of these things, because on the day that I gave my two-week notice, July 5, I was actually scared out of my mind. My job had been a safety net for a very long time. Once I quit, there would be no going back. I was about to embark on the great unknown. Also, I felt oddly worried about my boss's reaction. Apparently, my fear of rejection ran so deep that I was actually concerned that she'd *reject* my quitting. I didn't want to upset her. But I knew I had to do it.

So I visualized the drawer filled with dusty blueprints—and mustered enough courage to knock on her office door.

Once inside, I stumbled through my rehearsed speech, telling her about my dream of becoming an entrepreneur. "If I don't do it now, I will never do it," I told her, almost pleading for her to understand and not get upset. The speech was a far cry from Jerry Maguire's.

My boss was visibly shocked. She stared at me for what felt like minutes, and I wondered what she was thinking. She was probably contemplating what kind of insanity had come over me, that I would give up a nice income and quit my job right before having a baby. I didn't want her to think ill of me, which felt like a kind of rejection. But I didn't know what else to say, so I just sat there, shifting around uncomfortably.

Eventually, she found her voice. "Oh my God!" she yelled. "Who's going to take on all your projects now? We just had a hiring freeze. Now what do I do?" I'd been afraid of her rejection, but it was clear that she had other things on her mind.

Soon after that, I started telling my friends that I'd quit my job, feeling a little surprised each time by my own words. When I made the announcement to everyone who came to our baby shower, there was an awkward silence. Instead of a pin drop, I think I actually heard a chopstick drop.

Two weeks after quitting, I walked out of that mammoth office building for the last time—saying good-bye to my salary, health benefits, 401(k), and my air-conditioned office. All my comforts—and all my excuses for not living my dream—grew smaller and smaller in the rearview mirror. I felt excited and free, but also scared. Tracy was scheduled to deliver my son, Brian, in four days.

*Holy crap*, I said to myself. *This is for real. I'd better not screw it up.*

There is no manual for building the Next Big Thing, but every start-up begins with an idea. I had been mulling one over for a while, something I believed in and that was better—and more sophisticated—than wheels on shoes. For a while, I'd been thinking about how and why people keep their promises. People make casual promises to friends, family members, and coworkers every day. What if I could develop an app that would issue some kind of points or credit for fulfilling a promise? "Gamifying" promises could potentially motivate people to keep their word, improve their relationships, and generate fun in the process. I'd spoken with plenty of friends about the idea, as well as several entrepreneurs whom I admire, and the majority of them liked the idea. Some talked to me about it for hours. Their feedback told me that I was onto something and gave me the confidence to finally—*finally!*—try turning one of my entrepreneurial ideas into a reality.

On the same day that I quit my job, I started looking for people to help me create the app. Specifically, I needed top-notch software engineers with the programming skills to write the code. (In the software start-up world, I was considered a "nontech" founder, meaning I had the idea and business expertise but didn't have the killer programming skills needed to write the app myself.) So I started recruiting. I asked everyone I knew for potential leads. When I ran out of acquaintances, I approached strangers at meetups and even at local basketball courts. When I ran out of in-person options, I hopped onto Craigslist and LinkedIn.

My frenetic efforts paid off. Within weeks, I'd assembled an international team of whip-smart engineers. The first was Vic, who was finishing his master's in computer science and already had a job offer from IBM. If I could dream it, Vic could code it. The second person was Chen, a computer science PhD candidate who specialized in programming algorithms and read advanced software architecture theory for fun. Then there was Brandon, who lived in Utah and was literally a hacker. In high school he sold his own hacking software for profit. Later, he dropped out of college after his own small mobile app company became successful enough to support him. The last person, Vijay, was an engineer in India and a former colleague of mine. We'd never met in person, but I knew him to be a hard worker and a master at coding.

I was very proud of my team and honored that they believed in my vision and were willing to jump on board. Soon after hiring them, I rented space in a coworking facility—specifically designed for entrepreneurs—in downtown Austin, and we got to work. Building the app, and the business, was hard, complicated, and required long hours, week after week. But I was having the time of my life.

I was amazed by how fast a team of capable engineers could build software. We blazed our way through five iterations of product development. In three months, we built a web app and an iPhone app that felt intuitive and fun. We started using the app among ourselves and were surprised by how much our desire to keep score of our promises to one another boosted our productivity. Of course, it's one thing for an app's inventors to love it. Getting outside customers to engage with a new app—in a landscape filled with mobile apps—was a much tougher sell. Thousands of apps get launched every day, and we were competing with all of them for attention. Still, it was evident we had a good concept on our hands. It might not become an instant hit, but I knew we could make it work given a bit more time.

But we needed money. Tracy and I had been married for two years by that time, and we were big savers. I had invested most of our savings in kick-starting my new venture. As personnel and operation costs piled up, those funds started dwindling. I couldn't invest more without putting a huge strain on our finances, especially with a newborn child. Tracy had given me six months—and I needed to start showing traction to justify our investment.

Four months into the journey, it looked like my prayer was about to be answered. Our promises app had attracted the interest of an outside investor. I spent hours preparing and scripting our pitch. The team practiced it together over and over again, as if we were rehearsing for the reality TV show *Shark Tank*. The pitch couldn't have gone better, at least in our minds. Afterward, we high-fived each other in celebration. And then the waiting began—the most agonizing wait I'd ever experienced.

It wasn't the first time that I'd had the tense experience of waiting for others to decide my fate. When I was fifteen, I waited for weeks for the U.S. Embassy in Beijing to decide whether to grant me a visa so that I could come to the United States (I got it). When I was seventeen, I waited for BYU to decide whether to offer me the scholarship that would mean I could afford school on my own (I got it). When I was twenty-five, I waited for an admission letter from Duke Business School (I got it). When I was twenty-eight, I waited for the yes from Tracy after proposing to her in front of four hundred classmates (the best yes of my life). Those were nerve-racking moments, with life-changing decisions hanging in the balance. But I don't know why, in terms of anxiety level, they paled in comparison to waiting for this investment decision.

I still believed that I was destined to become a great entrepreneur. But I had just two months left to save my dream, and this investment felt like a lifeline. I wanted it so badly that I actually dreamed about getting a yes from the investor five different times, each time waking up thinking that the investment had come through. I vividly remember picking up the phone and calling my wife and family to tell them the good news in those dreams.

Several days later I was at a restaurant, attending a friend's birthday party, when my phone vibrated. It was an e-mail from the investor. My hand started to shake, and an ominous feeling engulfed me.

I held the phone for a long time without opening the e-mail, trying to channel all kinds of positive mental energy into its content. Then I clicked it open. It was a very short e-mail. The investor said no.

CHAPTER 2

# FIGHTING REJECTION

**I**HANDED MY PHONE TO TRACY SO THAT SHE COULD READ the e-mail; then I excused myself from the table and walked outside. All around me, diners were leaving the restaurant, and new groups were coming in. I could hear my friends singing "Happy Birthday" inside. Just like on July 4, I felt like a lonely, sad person adrift in a sea of other people's happiness. Before, I had failed to take a risk. Now, I had taken a risk and failed.

I stood there in the parking lot for a good fifteen minutes, trying to control my emotions. Eventually I returned to the table, but I don't think I said another word at the party. Tracy later told me that I looked like the kid from *The Sixth Sense* who was seeing dead people.

For months, I'd been driving to work each day feeling uplifted—like a man finally living his destiny. But the day after the investor turned us down, everything felt different. My drive felt depressing, and the traffic unbearable. Our co-working office space, which I'd grown to love, no longer felt inviting. Even the usually cheerful office manager somehow didn't seem friendly anymore. I had been rejected. My dream had been rejected. And it hurt.

Success no longer seemed like the sure outcome. In fact, it didn't seem probable or even plausible anymore. I started doubting my idea: *The investor is an entrepreneurial veteran. If he thinks my company is not worth investing in, there must be some truth to it.*

I started doubting myself, too: *Who do you think you are? Who told you that you were ordained to be a successful entrepreneur? You are living a childish dream. Welcome to reality, my friend! Start-up success is for special geniuses like Bill Gates and Steve Jobs. You are just like everybody else—a wannabe.*

Then I started getting angry with myself: *What the hell were you doing? How foolish were you, giving up a good job and diving headfirst into an unknown venture?*

I also felt sorry for Tracy, convinced that I had let her down and that she'd be so disappointed in me. *You see how painful that was? Are you going to go through all that and get rejected again? No way!*

Finally, I started getting scared: *Now what? What are your friends going to say? Your in-laws? They probably think you're irrational and an irresponsible husband and father—and maybe you are.*

The problem with insecurity is that you start feeling like everyone might reject you, even your closest loved ones. My first day back at the start-up after the investor's rejection was dismal. When I got home that night, I felt compelled to apologize to Tracy. I told her I was sorry that I'd failed, and that I was beginning to think that the start-up life wasn't for me. I suggested that I might cut my losses and start looking for a new job a few weeks earlier than I'd planned, so that we could get the income flowing again.

When I finished talking, I looked at Tracy, expecting her to walk over and hug me in sympathy. Instead, I got a wake-up call. "I gave you six months, I didn't give you four," she said. "You have two months left. Keep going and leave no regret!" I was ready to give up, but Tracy had another idea. She was fired up, like a pissed-off quarterback who grabs the offensive lineman's face mask and screams into it after he gives up a sack. It was another "I realized I married up" moment.

I agreed that I would stick it out for two more months—and that during that time I would do everything in my power to lift my idea and my company off the ground.

But the funding debacle had left me terrified of the next rejection. I wanted to pursue other investors, but I felt stuck in fear that they'd all say no and my dream would die. When I looked at myself in the mirror, I saw an ambitious guy who couldn't handle rejection. I'd spent years working in a safe corporate environment and hiding from risks inside a team. I wasn't used to putting myself out there. If I really wanted to be an entrepreneur, I needed to get better at dealing with *no*. Would Thomas Edison, Konosuke Matsushita, or Bill Gates have wanted to quit after only four months? No way!

I had two months to improve the app and find additional investment. But I realized that I also needed to find a way to become stronger when facing rejection. I needed not just to overcome my fear of no but to learn how to thrive in the face of it. If I was David, then rejection was my big, hairy Goliath. I needed to find the right tools, the right armor, and the right slingshot and stone to take him down.

I started with the most high-tech weapon in my arsenal: Google. I typed "overcoming rejection" into the search box and quickly scanned the results: a how-to article, a bevy of psychology articles, and a smattering of inspirational quotes. None of them called out to me as a solution to my problem. I wasn't interested in counseling or bits of inspiration. I wanted action.

After meandering through a series of links, I stumbled upon a website devoted to something called Rejection Therapy—a game of sorts developed by a Canadian entrepreneur named Jason Comely, in which you purposely and repeatedly seek out rejection to desensitize yourself to the pain of the word *no*. For some reason, I fell in love with the idea. It reminded me of the ancient Iron Fist technique in kung fu, where a person repeatedly pummels hard objects with his or her fist to gain resistance to pain.

Maybe I've seen too many kung fu movies, but the idea of overcoming rejection by throwing myself at it again and again and again held an odd sort of appeal. This was exactly what I needed—an Iron Fist approach to rejection. In an over-the-top move reminiscent of my teenage promise to conquer Microsoft, I made a vow not only to try rejection therapy but to do it one hundred times, video-record the entire experience, and start a blog on the topic. I found a domain name called FearBuster.com. There I would start my blog, which I called "100 Days of Rejection." I had never blogged before. But I liked the built-in accountability that blogging seemed to promise. If I managed to get any followers, then it would be hard to quit halfway.

Comely's game sells a deck of cards preloaded with tasks that players can do each day that will likely lead to a no— things like "Friend a complete stranger on Facebook" or "Ask for directions from someone on the street." But to me, these sounded too tame. If I was going to do this, then I wanted my rejection attempts to be creative, maybe even a little bit crazy. I also wanted them to be uniquely my own. I figured this might inject a little fun into a task that pretty much terrified me.

The next day, my rejection journey began.

## 100 DAYS OF REJECTION: DAY 1

Almost the whole day went by without me making a single move. Starting wasn't easy, both because rejection was something I dreaded and because I didn't have a clear idea of what I should be trying to get. Then, as I was walking through the lobby of my office building that evening, I noticed the security guard sitting at his desk. An idea popped into my head. What would happen if I tried to borrow $100 from him? As soon as I asked myself the question, I could feel all the hair on the back of my neck standing up. It seemed a certainty that the security guard would say no—and, in fact, that was the whole point. But *how* would he say no? Would he cuss me

out? Laugh at me? Whip out his nightstick and start club-
bing me? Would he think I was a nutcase and call the nearest
mental hospital asking if any six-foot-tall Asian male patient
had gone missing—all while holding me in a headlock? And
wait a second—did this guy have a gun or a Taser?

All these questions stormed into my mind, getting cra-
zier and darker by the second. So before I could scare myself
to death, I decided to just ask the damn question and see
what happened. I pulled out my phone, hit the video recording button, and aimed the camera at myself. "All right, this is
my first try. I'm going to try to borrow $100 from a stranger.
Ah . . . this is really tough, but let's give it a shot."

With my phone held up and recording, I started walking
toward the security guard, who was reading a newspaper.

"Excuse me," I said, my heart pounding like I'd just
downed five cups of coffee.

He glanced up, and before he could say anything at all,
I rushed in with my question. "Do you think I can borrow
$100 from you?"

He frowned. "No. Why?"

"No? All right. No? OK, thanks!" I said, fumbling my
words. I felt a rush of white noise in my ears. Then I left as
fast as I could, feeling like some sort of small animal running away from a predator that was still deciding whether to
chase me or let me go.

I went to a corner of the building and sat down to calm
myself. Some people would probably wonder what the big
deal was. But for me, being rejected for money felt like an
epic blend of failure and shame. I'd come to America as
an immigrant, been educated at good schools, and worked

for good companies. I was proud of the social status I had earned over the years. Asking a stranger for money was hard enough; getting turned down was almost too much for me, even as a made-up rejection attempt.

*Man, this stinks*, I said to myself. I hoped my father didn't watch the video—or worse, my uncle. I wouldn't want them to see me even pretending to panhandle. But this was rejection therapy, after all, and therapy is supposed to be painful. I left the building and hoped that I could cope better the next time.

That night, as I was editing the video before uploading it to YouTube and to my video blog, I got a whole new perspective on the experience. I could see in the video how terrified I was. When I was talking to the camera before my request, I looked like the guy in Edvard Munch's painting *The Scream*, only with a forced smile and some hair on my head. If I was that scared, I wonder what the security guard saw and how he felt.

Then I watched the next part, where I asked the question and the security guard answered. He'd said "No," but then he'd asked "Why?"—giving me a chance to explain myself. I'd been so frazzled by posing the question that I hadn't really heard his full response. Maybe he was intrigued by my bizarre request. Maybe he saw how scared I looked and thought I was in some sort of trouble. In any case, he was offering to extend the conversation. I could have said, in all honesty, "I'm trying to overcome my fear of rejection, so I am forcing myself to make absurd requests." Or "I'm trying to see if I can make something impossible happen. If you could trust me and lend me $100, I will give it back to you right away. I work upstairs. Here is my driver's license if that helps." I could have said so many things to at least make myself look reasonable and put him at ease.

But what did I say? "No? All right. No? OK, thanks!" All I wanted was to get out of there as soon as I could. Watching the conversation replayed on video in front of me, all I could think was: *What a wasted opportunity*. Fear had turned me into a mumbling idiot.

As I thought about what I was going to post, I also had to wonder: Why had I been so scared? The security guard didn't look menacing or intimidating at all—and definitely not like someone who would pummel me with a nightstick for asking a question. But I'd approached him as if he were a starving tiger. My goal had been to get a rejection, and I got what I wanted. So why was it still such a frightening moment?

I didn't have the answers. But I did know that my fear had a negative impact on the result. I decided to go into the next day's rejection attempt with a different approach. This time, I wanted to show a little confidence and composure during my encounter and see if I got the same outcome. I wanted to be able to sustain a conversation and explain myself. I even wanted to inject a little humor into my request—if that was at all possible.

## 100 DAYS OF REJECTION: DAY 2

It was lunchtime the next day. I was starving, so I went to Five Guys Burgers and Fries and ordered a big, juicy bacon cheeseburger. After gobbling the burger in just a few bites, my taste buds were begging me to order another one. I'd purchased a soda with my burger, and when I was filling my cup, I'd noticed a sign on the soda machine that said FREE REFILL. Suddenly, I had an idea for another rejection attempt. This time, I didn't give myself a chance to overthink the request and psych myself out. I whipped out my iPhone, hit record, and approached the cashier.

"What can I do for you?" the cashier asked.

I straightened my stance, poked my chest out a little, and made direct eye contact. "Your burger is really good. Can I get a burger refill?"

"Ah, ah, ah . . . what?" The cashier stuttered a little, trying to confirm what he thought he'd just heard. So I repeated my request.

"A burger refill? What do you mean?" he said, looking completely perplexed.

"Like, a free refill. Do you have free refills for burgers?" I tried to sound matter-of-fact and breezy, like I was asking a totally reasonable question.

The cashier said no. But instead of walking away this time, I asked a follow-up question—while trying not to laugh at the absurdity of what I was asking. "How come you have it for drinks but not for burgers?"

"That's the way it is, man," the cashier said, this time with a chuckle.

I told him I'd like the place even more if they offered a burger refill, then smiled and left.

That night, while readying the video for upload, I analyzed the conversation. I saw how my behavior had changed this time. I still looked a bit nervous, but that life-and-death panic hadn't kicked in. Neither had the wave of shame I'd experienced the day before in the lobby. Most important, I'd even had a little fun. And when I got the rejection, I was able to carry on a conversation without fleeing the scene. I even got a smile out of the cashier.

Two days into my rejection journey, I had already learned my first big lesson: the way you ask a question—and how you follow through in the conversation—has an impact on the result you get. It might not change the outcome, but it can take a lot of the sting out of hearing no. Projecting confidence and staying calm—rather than cowering—had created a totally different experience. If I could build up that sort of confidence in my professional life, rejection might not have such a devastating impact on my trajectory. It also might not hurt so much.

It had been only two days, and I was already feeling a little bit tougher. And now that my panic was subsiding, my creativity had started flowing again. I felt more like myself and a little bit less afraid of hearing the word *no*.

## 100 DAYS OF REJECTION: DAY 3

The next morning, I was stuck in traffic and thinking about how to get rejected that day when I spotted a Krispy Kreme shop on the side of the road. This was the same year as the 2012 London Olympics, and the Games were on my mind. So I came up with an outlandish rejection idea to try out in the donut shop on my way home that evening. I would ask them to make me five donuts, interlinked in the shape of the

Olympic rings. They'd say no, and I'd buy a box of donuts and head home, winning a rejection and a sweet treat in the process.

I left work a little early and drove to the Krispy Kreme. I was strangely looking forward to being rejected this time, maybe because there was a promise of donuts on the other end. I started recording myself while I was driving, to set up the "episode" for my video blog. When I got to the donut shop, it was bustling with customers. Standing in line, I practiced a few preplanned jokes in my head and coached myself to be calm, confident, and respectful. On the video, I can hear myself whispering, *"Everything will be OK."* I tried to visualize myself as a Chinese version of Bill Clinton, the most charismatic guy I could think of, hoping it would boost my confidence.

Finally, it was my turn. The cashier—who turned out to be the shift leader—looked to be in her forties. She had blond hair pulled into a ponytail under a Krispy Kreme baseball cap.

"How can I help you?" she asked.

I flashed what I hoped was a Clinton-like presidential smile. Then I asked my question: "Can you make me some specialized donuts?"

"What kind of specialized donuts are you talking about?"

"Ah, I'd like to have a . . ." I stumbled for a second, looked downward, then glanced up at the menu on the wall, as if there were an actual item called "Olympic Donuts."

I took a breath, forced myself to reestablish eye contact, and dove in. "Can you link the five donuts together and make them look like the Olympic symbol?"

She cocked her head and put her hand underneath her chin and let out a surprised "Oh!"

And that's when things got interesting.

"When are you looking for these?" she asked after a couple of seconds.

"Huh?" I muttered, as if I didn't understand her reply. Her question caught me completely off guard.

"When?" she repeated.

I paused for a second. I had counted on her saying no, so that I could then tell her why I was asking, deliver my jokes, and go home. But she had asked me "when" as if she were going to take me seriously.

"In the next . . . fifteen minutes?" I said, hoping the tight time frame would push her toward a quick no.

She looked away, still with her hand under her chin, and started thinking.

Then she pulled out paper and a pen. In the next few minutes, we went back and forth on what the donuts would look like. She started jotting down notes and drawing the rings on a piece of paper. She thought out loud about how she could make these donuts with Krispy Kreme's donut proofer and fryer.

Then, with the look of an Olympic athlete determined to win gold, she looked at me and said, "Let me see what I can do." Then she disappeared into the kitchen.

I found a seat and waited for my order. *Is this really happening?* I kept asking myself. I had come here to make a ridiculous request and get a no. Now here I was, dumbfounded by her equally ridiculous yes.

My phone rang. It was Tracy, asking me when I would be

home. Dinner was ready. "You'll have to wait for a few more minutes," I told her. "Remember my 100 Days of Rejection?"

"Yeah . . ." she said slowly, clearly wondering what sort of trouble I'd landed in.

"Something amazing is happening," I said. "I will explain it to you when I get home. Trust me, it's worth the wait."

A few minutes later, the woman strode out from the kitchen with a donut box in her hands. Inside were five interlinked donuts, each "ring" of donut iced in its appropriate color. There was no mistaking what they looked like: the Olympic rings.

"Wow!" I said. "That is really good. Really good!" It was then that I noticed her name tag, which read "Jackie." I later found out that her full name is Jackie Braun, and she's from New York.

"Jackie," I said. "I'm a fan!"

She told me I was too kind, then flashed a huge smile, the type you see only on someone who's made another person happy.

I was willing to pay whatever she asked for the donuts and began to pull out my wallet. But then Jackie surprised me again. "Don't even worry about it. This one is on me."

I couldn't believe it. I asked her twice if she was serious. She was.

I didn't know how to thank her. I went to shake her hand, but somehow my gesture turned into a full-blown hug.

On the drive home, I kept looking over at the box of donuts sitting on the passenger seat. It wasn't every day I experienced—or even heard of—the kind of awesome customer service and human kindness that Jackie had demonstrated.

I'd heard plenty of news stories about fighting, theft, corporate greed, and low food quality at fast-food restaurants. But fast-food managers willing to fill an absurd specialty order in under fifteen minutes? Now that was remarkable!

Even more remarkable: my rejection attempt had been rejected. I hadn't needed to pull out my jokes, explain myself, or channel Bill Clinton—I didn't have to do anything but muster the courage to ask the question to get a yes. Jackie and I had collaborated to turn my crazy idea into reality, and we'd had a lot of fun stepping outside the box of our otherwise average days. If I hadn't asked the question, I would never have experienced this moment. The Olympic ring donuts would have never been made, and Jackie would never have had the opportunity to please a customer in an unexpected way. Driving home, I couldn't help feeling that the world was actually much kinder, and its people much nicer, than I had realized.

I was brimming with excitement. I hadn't felt this way since I was a child. It wasn't the quick rush you get when playing a prank or the surge of adrenaline that follows a surprise victory. It was . . . possibilities. A sense that the world was filled with far more possibilities than I had imagined. If I could get custom-made Olympic donuts from Krispy Kreme without even trying, what else was possible if I just asked? A better question: What was possible if I really tried hard?

When I got home, I showed Tracy the video. She was as stunned as I had been and let out a big "Wow." After eating dinner (which had long gone cold), we dove into our unexpected dessert: the Olympic donuts. The icing was very sweet—but the feeling they created was far sweeter.

After dinner, I uploaded the video to YouTube and my video blog, along with some comments expressing my thoughts about the encounter. I wanted to share the story with the world; I wanted to let people know about an amazing donut maker in Austin who took her job seriously and made my day, and I also wanted to show people what was possible with a little bit of bravery and creativity. I was hoping a few hundred viewers might see the video. And that maybe, after watching the video, they would trust others a little more and open up a little more. Maybe.

In the Bible, the story goes that Apostle Paul started as a tormentor of Christians, persecuting and killing many early followers of Jesus. On the road to Damascus, he had a personal encounter with Jesus and experienced one of the most dramatic and eventful conversions in the history of religion. Paul went on to become an influential Christian missionary. His work and writings literally altered human history, accelerating the spread of Christianity to the point that the Roman Empire adopted it as its dominant religion.

I am no Apostle Paul, and Jackie from Krispy Kreme is no Jesus. But my visit to Krispy Kreme felt like my own version on the road to Damascus. My entire worldview was altered, and I felt almost like a new person. My first and second rejection attempts had changed my perspective—but my third attempt had transformed my mind-set. Before Jackie, I hadn't even considered the possibility that people might say yes to one of my requests. But as a result of that experience, my focus now shifted from getting a rejection and just coping

with the ensuing pain to having the courage to make big requests. I stopped caring so much whether I got a yes or a no.
Which meant, I supposed, that I was starting to care a bit
less about what other people thought about me. And it felt
liberating.

## 100 DAYS OF REJECTION: DAYS 4–6

The next day, I went into a Domino's pizza shop and asked if
I could deliver a pizza for them as a volunteer deliveryman.
The day after, I asked a grocery store clerk if he could give
me a tour of their warehouse. The answer to both requests
was no—but I didn't take it personally. I felt confident and
relaxed, and I was having fun.

I also felt like it was time to intensify the challenge. So
far, the people I'd approached had been at their workplaces.
They basically had to talk to me, because dealing with customers was part of their jobs. What if, I mused on my way
home from work one day, I started seeking rejection from
people who had no reason to talk to me at all? I felt the hair at
the back of my neck spring up again at the very thought. But
I wanted to force myself to be uncomfortable. And that's how
I came up with rejection attempt number six: knocking on
a stranger's door and asking to play soccer in his backyard.

When I lived in other parts of the country, and witnessed
(or did) something that could be perceived as abnormal or
dangerous, I'd often heard the phrase "In Texas, you'd get
shot for that." Well, Austin was the capital of the you-would-
get-shot-for-that state. And, with request number six, I was
asking to invade a random Texan's personal space—which

didn't sound like a good idea even in the best of circumstances. And that's why, when I stood at the Dallas Cowboys fan's front door, sweating through my soccer gear and waiting for his response, I couldn't help but wonder: *Will I come out of this rejection attempt in one piece?*

Scott, the Cowboys fan, had taken a few moments to respond to my bizarre request. But then he'd cocked a slight smile and said, "I guess so."

The five minutes that followed were a total blur: walking through this stranger's house into his backyard, bouncing the ball off my foot in the grass, and posing for a picture. I wasn't sure which one of us was more confused by the moment, but I was grateful to Scott for playing along. On my way out, I couldn't help but ask him why he'd said yes.

Scott rubbed his chin. "Well, it was so off the wall, how could I say no?"

*How could I say no?*

These words stuck in my mind like a catchy billboard top 10 song. After Krispy Kreme, I knew I would get more yeses. But a yes from a die-hard football fan who would agree to miss watching overtime so that he could snap a picture of a stranger playing soccer in his yard? Despite having absolutely no reason or incentive to say yes, he'd been compelled to oblige because of—not in spite of—the fact that my request was so outrageous.

There's no doubt that not everyone would say yes to me like Scott did. But Scott taught me that sometimes personal curiosity on the part of the person on the receiving end of the question could dictate the outcome. And that by piquing the other person's interest with the way I made the request, I might have a higher probability of getting a yes.

Jason Comely's original rejection game is about pain desensitization. But my 100 Days of Rejection experiment was quickly turning into something very different—a crash course on life and business. I was starting to see just how important my communication style was to the outcomes I was getting. When I was confident, friendly, and open, people seemed more inclined to go along with my request; even if they said no, they at least stayed engaged longer to ask questions. If I could just figure out the right way to communicate in each situation, I might increase my chance of being accepted—and also decrease my fears about a possible rejection.

Maybe rejection was much less black and white than it seemed—it wasn't just about being in the right place at the right time to get what I wanted or not. Maybe there were things I could do to influence or even change the outcome. For any one rejection, many variables were in play, including who was asking, who was being asked, what was being asked, how it was asked, how many times it was asked, and where it was asked. Maybe it's like an equation: by changing any of these factors, the outcome would be completely different. In the evenings, I found myself lying in bed thinking about my past and wondering how my results might have been different if I had realized some of these things earlier.

When I was twenty-five, I applied and got into my dream business school, aiming to learn everything I could about business so that someday I could become a leader and an

entrepreneur. About $80,000 of student loan debt later, I'd
learned a lot of business theories and become a master of
spreadsheets and PowerPoint decks. Now, less than a week
into my rejection journey, I felt I'd already learned more
about business and human psychology than I ever had in
business school.

And something else was starting to change: my confidence and demeanor.

Less than a week after I approached the security guard
asking for $100, I started noticing changes in how I carried
myself and how I moved through the world. I was still working with my start-up team, and we were still trying to lift our
app off the ground. But instead of approaching my leadership of the company with a vague sense of dread, I felt more
engaged than ever. I was smiling a little more and conducting meetings with more poise. I offered my opinions more
freely, without constantly studying other people's faces to see
if they liked what I was saying. I asked for feedback without searching for praise and got a little better at not taking
criticism personally. Without the negative emotion I usually
attached to it—hearing criticism in any comment—the feedback became much more useful. I felt like I was becoming
a leader who asked, listened, and inspired, instead of just a
person who gave directions. My confidence soared.

The changes weren't just happening in my business life,
either. As I became more aware of how my demeanor impacted the world around me, I was also becoming much
more clear and deliberate in my conversations with my wife
and with friends. Within the first few weeks of my 100 Days,
several people told me that I seemed different somehow,

more sure of myself. Even my in-laws started looking at me differently, with something that felt like the beginnings of respect.

It felt like the start of the kind of magical transformation that people talk about in those late-night infomercials for self-improvement products. I had always believed in working hard to pursue my dreams and had never put much stock in life-transformation stories. But now, it seemed, I was actually beginning to live one myself. I was discovering something new, exciting, and useful. And I couldn't wait to see what I would learn next.

But then something happened and interrupted everything I was doing and learning.

Fame.

CHAPTER 3

# TASTING FAME

**S**INCE I'D STARTED RECORDING AND POSTING MY REJEC-
tion attempts, the traffic on my website had steadily increased. My Krispy Kreme adventure was especially popular;
it got hundreds of views soon after I posted it.

Then someone posted the Krispy Kreme video on Reddit
.com, a social news and entertainment website where users
can submit web content, and others can vote up and down
based on whether they like it. The most liked content gets
featured on Reddit.com's homepage, exposing it to thousands more viewers. My video—submitted by someone with
the username "BHSPitMonkey" under the title "Man tried
making strange requests in order to get rejected; awesome
doughnut shop manager steps up to the challenge"—quickly
caught fire. It generated more than 15,000 "up" votes and
stayed on Reddit's front page for two straight days. It also

drew more than 1,200 comments, most of them from people gushing over Jackie:

> "She transcended her position in life. Very inspiring."
> —userofthissite

> "She's my hero. I'm a manager at a pizza place and this stuff gets to me."—Ghostronic

> "I teared up when she didn't charge. I should be a better person."—HectorCruzSuarez

There were also a lot of comments about Krispy Kreme as a company:

> "This definitely improved my image of Krispy Kreme, even though I know they don't employ a clone army of Jackies at every location yet."—anonymous

> "This woman did way more for Krispy Kreme than giving those donuts away, this PR is priceless for a company."
> —ubrpwnzr

> "I've always been impressed by Krispy Kreme."
> —Wingineer

There were heartfelt comments about customer interaction and customer service:

> "When I worked retail I always liked challenging questions like this (if you're nice about it, that is). Seriously, any chance to think a little more deeply about something made my day."—mollaby38

> "This is the kind of customer service that not only keeps
> a customer loyal, it keeps them returning and telling
> others to go there."—Peskie

> "She just seemed so happy, I bet it made her day,
> maybe even made her week. A difference in your
> routine can make a huge difference."—Benny0_o

And it wasn't just Jackie and Krispy Kreme drawing attention. People had comments about me, too:

> "The real point is that if he takes some risks and puts
> himself out there, he won't get rejected as often as he
> expects and there's even a chance that some awesome
> things will happen."—demilitarized_zone

> "I think the fact this woman wanted to help him should
> end any fears he has of rejection."—unknown

> "Definitely would befriend a guy who's willing to
> overcome his fears by putting himself in funny situations
> where he's gotta confront it head on."—MrMiday

Reddit was only the beginning. The following week, the story was picked up worldwide. Yahoo! News put the video on its front page. Gawker, MSN.com, the Huffington Post, the UK's *Daily Mail*, and the *Times of India* quickly followed suit. Overnight, the Krispy Kreme video became an international sensation with millions of views.

Krispy Kreme suddenly got the kind of publicity marketers only dream about. Calls flooded into their national headquarters and the Austin store, praising Jackie Braun. The company itself publicly honored Jackie with a tweet: "Yes, well done Jackie! #heartjackie." Clearly, the story had struck a nerve. And it seemed that this little act was not just warming hearts all around the world. It might also have come with some real financial benefits. The week after the video went viral, Krispy Kreme's stock price leapt from $7.23 to $9.32. Of course, I have no scientifically proven way to attribute a 29 percent stock price jump worth hundreds of millions of dollars to a single video. But I am sure it didn't hurt.

I was sitting in a coffee shop doing work on the day the story caught fire. All of sudden my phone started vibrating like mad. Friends and family were practically screaming into the phone and flooding my in-box with e-mails. Media outlets like MSNBC, the *Steve Harvey Show*, Fox News, and radio stations I'd never heard of bombarded me with interview requests. They clogged my voice mail with messages urging me to call them back immediately so they could write about my story or book me on their shows. *Bloomberg Businessweek*—which happened to be one of my favorite magazines—even flew a reporter down from New York to interview me for a story they titled "The No Man." It made me feel like I was some sort of superhero.

The story also caught the interest of Hollywood. Almost overnight, reality TV producers started pitching me ideas about turning my story into a TV show, where I would be the rejection expert helping others overcome their fears and solve their life problems. One of them dubbed me the "Rejection Whisperer," after the bestselling novel *The Horse Whisperer*, and the popular dog-training reality TV show *The Dog Whisperer* with Cesar Millan. And I was even approached by a former movie executive who had somehow already written a script loosely based on my story, in which I was a depressed single guy who finally "finds himself"—and his true love— after 100 days of rejection. Never mind that I was a happily married man or that my 100 days had only just started.

People started to recognize me on the street. I was walking down the sidewalk one day when a driver slowed down his car, waved to me, and yelled out, "I love your video!" The next day, my wife and I were buying movie tickets when the ticket clerk started studying my face. She asked me if I was the person with all the "cool videos," and then she asked if she could take a picture with me. I said yes—I might be the "No Man," but I had better say yes to this kind of fan request! But I also felt dumbfounded, not just by her request, but by everything that was happening to me. What was it about this video that struck such a nerve with people?

These kinds of encounters went on and on. It's hard, even now, for me to believe that a video I'd created as a tool to help me overcome my fear of rejection—a video about customized donuts—somehow managed to catapult me into the spotlight in a way that I'd never intended and frankly never craved. I had imagined myself achieving some sort of fame as a by-product of building the next Microsoft or Google, not because I was trying to battle my fear of rejection.

And then it got even stranger.

## 100 DAYS OF REJECTION: HAVE A TV HOST
## SING TO MY SON

I have been a casual viewer of the show *Survivor* for years. I like it for its competition, characters, and good old reality TV drama. But more than anything else, I like its Emmy-winning host, Jeff Probst, and the way he interacts with contestants on a personal and compassionate level. So when the producer of the nationally syndicated *Jeff Probst Show* called and invited me to come on the show, I knew I had to say yes.

Two weeks later, CBS flew me to Hollywood. They also flew in Jackie Braun from Krispy Kreme. I have seen Jackie a few more times since that day, and every time I have been impressed by her humility and grace. In the greenroom before the show, while the makeup artists were getting us TV-ready, Jackie and I chatted about our strange journey—from a Krispy Kreme store in Austin to national television. Since the video had gone viral, hundreds of people had stopped by the Krispy Kreme where Jackie worked to meet her. She thanked me for giving her the chance to be appreciated by the public. But she also insisted that what she had done wasn't extraordinary, and that many of her coworkers would have done the same thing.

The producers had invited one more person to join us onstage: Jason Comely, the inventor of the Rejection Therapy game that had inspired my 100 Days of Rejection quest. I'd never met him before but liked him instantly, and we have since become good friends. He told me that my blog had brought a lot of traffic to his site and his business. He also confessed that he'd been going through a tough time of his own and was finding the videos and my story inspiring.

Our segment came after Danica Patrick, the racecar driver. I was surprised, given my outsized fear of rejection, that being on national television didn't scare me to death. Maybe it's because the one person in the world whose acceptance and recognition I crave above all others was in the studio audience that day. My uncle—the person who was my role model growing up and whom I named my son after, but whose rejection of my entrepreneurial idea fourteen years earlier had left me stunned and unsure of myself—had driven all the way from San Diego to watch me on the show. Seeing him in the audience, smiling his encouragement and beaming with pride, made me feel like the luckiest man in the world.

It also gave me the courage to launch another rejection attempt—right there on TV. At the end of our segment, I asked Jeff Probst to sing "Twinkle, Twinkle, Little Star" to my son. It was Brian's favorite song. Jeff not only did it, but he got the entire studio audience to sing with him. Afterward, Jeff shook my hand. "Congratulations," he said. "What you are doing is fabulous. You are onto something big here. Continue to inspire!"

All the attention from the media and from the public was pretty extraordinary. But if I had to pick one event that was the most unexpected, it was an e-mail reply from my personal hero.

I used to be very hesitant about contacting people through "cold calls" or "cold e-mails," because the chance of being ignored or rejected seemed overwhelming. And the possibility of being rejected by famous, busy people was close to 100 percent, at least in my mind. But the momentum of my videos gave me the courage to send a few e-mails to some of my role models. I desperately wanted to get some advice on running my fledgling start-up.

One of the people I e-mailed was Tony Hsieh, the CEO of Zappos, the popular online shoe retailer. I'd read his book *Delivering Happiness* over and over again for inspiration when I was working at my old job. The book shares his early dreams of becoming an entrepreneur and how he fulfilled those dreams by building LinkExchange and later Zappos, overcoming all kinds of obstacles in the process. As a fellow Asian entrepreneur, I could relate to his struggles and his ambition, and I badly wanted to have the same impact that he has had.

It's crazy what can happen if you just ask. To my shock, I received a reply from one of Tony's assistants. It turned out that Tony had heard about my story and liked my videos. He wanted to invite me to fly to Las Vegas, where Zappos is headquartered, to give a talk as part of his Las Vegas Downtown Project.

In 2012, Tony was working on revitalizing downtown Las Vegas, moving it out from the shadows of the Las Vegas strip and transforming it into a cultural and technology hot spot to rival Austin and San Francisco. The Downtown Project was all about inspiring local businesses to think of themselves as part of a larger vision, and he thought hearing my story might help them think bigger about their aspirations.

Tony Hsieh, an inspiration of mine, wanted to invite me to deliver inspiration?

A week later, I was in Las Vegas, giving my speech. The event was held in a temporary theater made out of construction trailers, designed to symbolize the rebuilding of the city. Las Vegas had been deeply hurt by the great recession. Housing values had plummeted by more than two-thirds. Many people who had come to the city during the boom were devastated by the bust, and some had simply moved away to start over somewhere else. Those who remained felt that their city had been rejected by the world and were struggling to keep their spirits high amid efforts to rebuild and revitalize.

On the stage, I shared my own dreams and struggles and talked about my rejection journey—from my decision to quit my job to pursue my childhood dream, to getting rejected by the investor and the magical experience I'd had so far during my 100 Days. I encouraged the audience not to give up, but to march forward and follow their dreams for the city and for themselves, no matter what anybody thought about them.

After the talk, the audience gave me a standing ovation—the first I had ever experienced in my life. I felt completely overwhelmed. Even more surreal, people surrounded me afterward, shaking my hand and thanking me for sharing my story, as if I was doing them a great favor by trying to tackle my own fear.

When the crowd started to thin, Tony Hsieh tapped my shoulder and invited me to his office for a private meeting.

Tony's story and achievements have made him a super-hero to aspiring entrepreneurs like me, so sitting in his office was a rather dreamlike experience. I wouldn't have been surprised if he'd thrown on an Iron Man suit and taken me for a ride. But after some small talk, Tony got down to business. He looked me in the eyes and asked: "How would you like to move to Las Vegas and work for me?"

On the flight from Las Vegas back to Austin, I watched out the window as the lights of the Las Vegas Strip shrank into the distance and then disappeared. The lights were replaced by total darkness; the only sound was the steady humming of the plane engine.

A few hours earlier, Tony Hsieh had offered me a job, or more like a business proposal. If I moved to Las Vegas, he would form a new business and hire me to work for it as a professional speaker. I would travel the country giving inspirational talks at conferences and corporations.

*So Tony Hsieh wants to hire me for a talent I never knew I had until today—in public speaking.*

The urge to say yes to whatever this man asked of me was so strong that I had almost agreed on the spot. But moving to Vegas and abandoning the company I had just formed was a decision that involved many more people than myself. So I'd asked for some time to consider the offer.

Now, sitting inside the plane, I had to ask myself: *What just happened?* Within a month, I'd gone from getting rejected by an investor, to asking for bizarre customized donuts, to being featured in newspapers, magazines, and national talk shows, to staring across a desk at Tony Hsieh, who was trying to convince *me* to come work for *him* on a national platform.

Was this another dream, like the ones I'd had before that investor turned me down? If so, I didn't know if I wanted it to keep going or to wake up.

But it wasn't a dream. And I had choices to make. Should I become the "Rejection Whisperer" on my own reality show? Play the depressed guy who finds true love through rejection therapy in a Hollywood movie? Work for my idol Tony Hsieh? Or go back to doing what I was doing—running a struggling tech start-up while video-blogging about rejection?

As much as I loved my start-up team and the app we were building, totally disregarding what had just opened up and going back to my routine seemed a little unwise if not crazy. Not everyone gets their fifteen minutes of fame, and mine had been pretty spectacular. If I wanted to capitalize on the new opportunities my "flash fame" had opened, then I needed to figure out which one of these new career paths would be the most meaningful in the long term. Maybe it was a combination of all of them.

As for Hsieh's invite, something about going back to working for someone else in his or her company didn't feel right. My goal in life has always been to make a positive impact in the world. Fame and celebrity had never been my main motive. So the idea of chasing after these flashy routes made me uneasy.

Also, I didn't feel ready for it. Basically, I was a guy with a cool story, and I had just learned that I could tell it pretty well. My rejection journey had just started yet I was already being seen as some sort of expert. It was as if I'd set out to climb Mount Everest and had only just set up my base camp, yet the world was already trying to helicopter me out and crown me a great adventurer. I still yearned to discover the rest of the mountain.

On the other hand, if I didn't jump on these opportunities now, would they still be there when I was ready for them?

I was getting a headache thinking about all this. To distract myself, I turned on my laptop and opened my e-mail box. There were more than one thousand unread messages waiting for me. Ever since the donut video had gone viral, my in-box had been brimming with "fan e-mails" from people all over the world. Some of them were light and funny, written by people who found my videos pretty amusing. Many of them—most, actually—were from people who had been taking the videos very seriously, using them as a way to gain courage to face their own rejection fears.

Like this e-mail from Mike:

> I have been following your 100 Days of Rejection
> Therapy almost from the beginning when my daughter
> sent me a link. Your journey has brought me many
> smiles, laughs, and strength. It is the strength that I
> have gained in my day to day activities that I want to
> thank you most for. Through my life, I have always
> found it difficult to approach people and ask the
> simplest questions, even of people whose job it is to
> help, like store clerks, wait staff, etc. At times I have
> even sent my children to ask for ketchup at McDonald's
> because the thought made my stomach knot up. . . .

This newfound strength has come at a very crucial time in my life. In May of last year, my wife was diagnosed with cancer and it has taken eight months of doctor and hospital visits to arrive at a final cancer type diagnosis. We have learned much about the inner workings of the healthcare system, both the good and the bad, and it all requires talking to many people and asking many questions. Every time I felt the fear of asking questions on our cancer journey, I thought of you and found the strength to step up and do what had to be done. Thanks so much for taking your journey and letting us all share and gain strength from your actions.

## And this one from Regina:

I am an actress working both out of NYC and Philadelphia and I really find this project fascinating because as an actor, we see more rejection in our work than most people. Every audition is like another job interview and the biggest fear is not booking that job or being rejected because someone else is "better." It is very easy to get discouraged and take it to heart. And in simple day to day scenarios, asking for simple things can make me break out in a sweat. I find while watching some of your videos on YouTube that I am squirming along with you, having to approach people and make a simple request.

In everyday situations for myself, the consequences conjured up by my imagination are far worse than what I think most outcomes will realistically be. Will someone

yell at me, or ridicule me, call me stupid, or throw me
out of their establishment? At an audition, will the
casting director stop me mid-performance and tell me
I have no talent and that the school that gave me my
MFA in Acting should not have given me a diploma?
My mind has some of the craziest ideas of potential
outcomes. And it is this fear of being rejected that can
paralyze people and keep them from really living. . . .
I cannot wait to see what other adventures you have.
I think you are learning a lot about rejection but even
more importantly, about how generous people can
be and the beauty of the human spirit. I know I am
learning so much by watching your project and about
staying positive. Good luck!

It's one thing to receive a few letters like this. But I'd been
getting hundreds of them—all from people who seemed just
as invested in my rejection journey as I was. I felt humbled
by their stories and honored to be helping them in some way
to face down their fears. But I was also amazed: Was I really impacting the lives of people I didn't know just by doing
what I was doing?

The media had come after me because of the entertainment value I could provide for them. "Guy seeks out rejection
but receives Olympic donuts instead" was perfect story-of-
the-day material. But the e-mails I was receiving from regular people—people just like me—were different. They didn't
see my journey as entertainment. It was almost as if they saw
me as representing them in some sort of struggle and had a
personal stake in seeing me succeed.

I'd always viewed my fear of rejection as some sort of rare disease, like guinea worm, that inflicts terrible pain but affects only a tiny segment of the overall population. I figured that I was simply unlucky, or that my innate shyness, my upbringing in a superprotective family, or the fact that I came from a foreign country with a reserved culture were somehow responsible for my fear. Before the e-mails and comments started pouring in, I'd never really thought about *other people's* fear of rejection. But the more people told me how much they could relate to my experience, the more I realized that fear of rejection wasn't a rare disease at all. It was a normal human condition.

I knew from experience that this fear can have enormous, debilitating consequences. Now I was hearing from people who, like me, viewed rejection as something so painful, so personal, and so negative that they would rather not ask for things, rather conform to the norm, and rather not take risks just to avoid the possibility of rejection. Like me, they had spent much of their lives rejecting themselves before others could get the chance. As a result, they had heartbreaking stories of ambitions that weren't fulfilled, job opportunities that were missed, love that was never realized—and inventions that were never made or were made by someone else. The worst part is that the "what ifs" that lingered in their minds were often caused by themselves, because they didn't even ask or didn't even try.

I once read a poignant memoir, *The Top Five Regrets of the Dying*, written by an Australian nurse named Bronnie Ware. She had interviewed dozens of terminally ill patients in hospice care and asked them about their deepest regrets.

The most frequent response she received was: "I wish I'd had the courage to live a life true to myself, not the life others expected of me."

What if we all had that courage? What if people didn't feel so trapped by their fear of rejection? What if rejection didn't feel so shameful and personal, but became more discussable? And what if we were able not just to talk about it, but to really figure out a way to conquer it?

If a person who fears rejection were suddenly unafraid of it, what might she be capable of? Wouldn't she be better at *everything* she does? If she were an artist or musician and didn't fear how people received her work, wouldn't she be able to search deep into her soul and make pieces that truly reflect who she is? If she were a salesperson, wouldn't she be able to call more prospects, follow up with more clients, and not get discouraged after a couple of nos? If she were a parent, wouldn't she be able to raise her children based on her principles rather than giving them whatever they wanted? Wouldn't a company or a nonprofit organization that didn't feel overly worried about shareholder reactions have the courage to innovate new products and services that could make the world a better place?

All my life, I'd wanted to be an entrepreneur. I'd wanted to invent something that millions of people would find useful. Yet by tackling one of my own needs head-on, I'd accidentally stumbled on a need so great that it was shared by most of the planet.

Paul Graham, the entrepreneur and founder of the famous start-up accelerator Y Combinator, once wrote: "The way to get startup ideas is not to try to think of startup ideas.

It's to look for problems, preferably problems you have your-self." All this time, I'd been focused on launching an app based on a cool idea in my head. But now, I saw far more meaning in helping people overcome their fear of rejection. I didn't know exactly what that would look like—or what it would mean for my own future—but the rest of my 100 Days of Rejection would be the perfect lab for me to experiment with a new kind of invention: a way to overcome the fear of rejection.

Reading the e-mails from Mike, Regina, and others had put my sudden blast of fame in perspective. When my plane landed in Austin-Bergstrom International Airport, I hurried down the aisle, eager to get back to my family and tell them about my decision. As I stepped out of the plane and into the tunnel, feeling the cold wind, I felt just like I had on my first day of college, when I'd walked across that vast field of untouched snow. Circumstances had just presented me with one of the greatest opportunities of my life. Everything felt new. Everything felt possible.

# CHAPTER 4

# BATTLING EVOLUTION

**M**AKING THE DECISION TO STOP BUILDING MY APP
and completely change direction wasn't easy, especially considering what I'd given up for that project and how
much I valued my team. But when I told them the news, they
were incredibly supportive. Like me, they'd been amazed by
the amount of publicity and traction my blog had received,
and they agreed that I'd stumbled on an even more meaningful endeavor. They felt like they'd contributed to it in a
roundabout way and were very proud of it. We agreed that
if I ever wanted to build technology related to the "rejection
problem," we would come back to work together again.

But now I had a new day job: confronting rejection full-
time.

Immediately, it became clear to me that if I was really
going to take on rejection on behalf of the world, then I

needed to supplement my rejection attempts with good old-fashioned research and learn as much about the topic as possible. I wanted to study this particular Goliath the way a sports team analyzes its opponent—by doing the equivalent of watching game tape, reading scouting reports, and practicing as much as I could before the real match.

My first online searches turned up almost nothing useful—mostly a swarm of inspirational quotes and superficial rah-rah talks by sales coaches and self-help gurus. Compared to related topics like success, charisma, leadership, negotiation, and even failure, I could find almost nothing that helped explain the subject of rejection and its relationship to our daily lives. What I found instead was a lot of advice that basically boiled down to this:

1. Rejection happens.
2. Don't take it personally.
3. Be tough and move on.

Well, sure—it would be great if everybody could operate that way. Our mainstream views on how to handle rejection are breathtakingly simplistic. Despite its prevalence and gut-wrenching consequence, we treat rejection as a one-off occurrence or temporary inconvenience—more like a bug bite or a flat tire than an experience that can shut down a person's ability to take risks forever. It's as if the subject were so simple that there was no need for more understanding. Didn't get the job or promotion? Couldn't close the sale? People thought your idea was stupid? The woman you love turns down your proposal? Don't take it personally! Dust yourself off and move on!

But if handling rejection were really that simple, why would a tabulation of Google search keywords, generated by billions of users, show that people rank rejection close to the top of their list of greatest fears, even above pain, loneliness, and illness? Why would people feel compelled to live up to others' expectations while ignoring their own, making failure to pursue their dreams one of their biggest regrets? Why would I bury the blueprints for my shoe-skate invention in the bottom of a drawer after my uncle scoffed at the idea, only to later witness Heelys's wild success?

Was I just weak? I didn't think so. I had traveled to a foreign country alone as a teenager, knowing absolutely nobody and speaking no English. I'd had to overcome all kinds of obstacles to learn a new language and become familiar with a new culture. I had worked hard to get where I was, against big odds. If I were weak, I probably would have headed back to China years ago, having put my entire dream of living and working in America into a drawer.

The thousands of people all over the world writing to me, expressing how much they feared rejection, couldn't be described as weak either. Experiencing a devastating rejection, such as losing a job you've held for decades, getting passed up for a promotion, or having your spouse push for a divorce when you don't want to quit the marriage can be life altering. For people in these situations, saying "don't take it personally" can feel insulting and ridiculous. But why does it bother us so much? The more I thought about it, the more I realized

I really had three burning questions: Why don't we talk about rejection more? Why is rejection so painful? And why do we fear rejection so much?

There had to be more to it than what my searches were telling me. Figuring that there must be better advice and wisdom out there, I kept looking for answers. I explored the fields of business, psychology, history, sociology, self-help, and behavioral economics for any insights I could find—to the point of obsession. After a few weeks of research, with my desk now piled high with books and articles and my in-box flooded with Google News Alerts on the subject of "rejection," I had taken tons of notes and was starting to feel like I was a professor in the school of rejection.

## REJECTION VS. FAILURE

Maybe the biggest reason people don't talk about rejection more is because they'd rather discuss its easier-to-manage conceptual cousin—failure. So many times, I'd start reading about rejection only to watch the text slide into a discussion of failure instead. But they aren't the same thing. When we fail at something, such as a business venture or a career, it feels unfortunate but understandable and often tolerable, because it could be due to a host of factors. It's easy to come up with reasons why something failed, whether they are logical reasons or simply excuses. If you fail at a business venture, you could reason that the idea was ahead of its time, that the market or the economy wasn't conducive to success, or that the idea wasn't well executed.

Even if it *was* your fault, there are all sorts of ways to turn failure into a positive. You could say "I simply wasn't good at it," vow to get better, or remind yourself of the thousands of other things you're amazing at. You could say "I made some mistakes"—because, after all, who doesn't? You could say "I learned a lot from this" and come out actually feeling better, more experienced, and wiser than before you failed. In Silicon Valley, entrepreneurs sometimes even wear their failures like badges of honor. The entire lean start-up movement was built on the concept of developing products by failing fast and learning from those failures.

In fact, entrepreneurs *love* to tell and hear stories about failure—because those letdowns are often stepping-stones toward eventual success. Business celebrities such as Donald Trump brag about having failed plenty before becoming the moguls they are today. We watch athletes and sports teams fail one week or one season only to triumph the next. Failure has almost become a prerequisite to success. In some cases, it could feel as cool as having street cred.

Rejection, on the other hand, is not cool at all. It involves another person saying no to us, often in favor of someone else, and often face-to-face. Rejection means that we wanted someone to believe in us but they didn't; that we wanted someone to like us but they didn't; we wanted them to see what we see and to think how we think—and instead they disagreed and judged our way of looking at the world as inferior. That feels deeply personal to a lot of us. It doesn't just feel like a rejection of our request, but also of our character, looks, ability, intelligence, personality, culture, or beliefs. Even if the person rejecting our request doesn't mean for his or her no to feel personal, it's going to. Rejection is an inherently unequal exchange between the rejector and the rejectee—and it affects the latter much more than it does the former.

When we experience rejection, we can't easily blame the economy, the market, or other people. If we can't deal with it in a healthy manner, we are left with two unhealthy choices. If we believe we deserved the rejection, we blame ourselves and get flooded with feelings of shame and ineptitude. If we believe the rejection is unjust or undeserved, we blame the other person and get consumed by feelings of anger and revenge.

Kevin Carlsmith, PhD, a social psychologist at Colgate University, set up lab experiments where the participants experienced a perceived injustice. Some of the individuals were given the choice to reap revenge on their wrongdoers, but others were not. Afterward, Carlsmith surveyed participants' feelings. Everyone who was given the chance to exact revenge took it. But everyone in the revenge group ended up feeling worse than the people who weren't given the choice. Interestingly, all the members of the no-revenge-choice group believed they would have felt better had they been given the chance to get back at their wrongdoers.

In other words, people naturally want revenge after they've been rejected, perhaps thinking that they will feel better by showing the rejectors how wrong they were. Yet it doesn't work that way, and those who lash out actually wind up feeling worse when they get revenge. This is just a small window into human nature in a safe lab environment. Yet in real life, we are inundated with unfortunate and even tragic incidences of school shooting and acid attacks, all due to people's desire for revenge after rejection.

## THE PAIN OF REJECTION

A few years ago, my wife, Tracy, and I took a fall trip to Italy. We'd been planning the trip for years, and it was supposed to be our dream vacation. Instead, two days into it, we had one of the worst vacation days we could imagine.

First, we got bad directions to the Colosseum and got hopelessly lost. Because of that miscue, we missed our bus to the countryside and had to scrap the idyllic daytrip we'd meticulously planned. Soon after, a street thug stole our camera—and with it, all our vacation pictures. It was as if the country of Italy had held a national conference before our arrival, at which the attendees devised ways to ruin our vacation.

It was after dusk, and we were walking back to our hotel, feeling exhausted and in terrible moods. Suddenly, Tracy bent forward and started wincing. For years, she'd had bouts of chronic stomach pain. The one she was experiencing now, in the middle of an Italian street, left her feeling like she was being stabbed. We didn't have any medicine with us and needed to buy some—as soon as possible. But we didn't know where to find it, or a single word of Italian.

It was 8:50 P.M., and most stores in Rome close at 9 P.M. We hurried to a nearby magazine stand. Luckily, it was still open. We hoped the person who worked at the stand could give us directions to the closest convenience store, supermarket, or shop that sold medicine.

Tracy stepped up to the stand's window and said, "Hello! Do you know where we can find . . ."

The women behind the window looked at us and said

"No" before Tracy could even finish asking her question. Then she stood up, pulled down the glass window, turned around, and started gathering her belongings. She closed the stand ten minutes early just so she would not have to bother talking to us.

I was furious. How could this woman treat Tracy this way? Couldn't she tell that my wife was in pain and we needed help? Was it because we were tourists who didn't speak Italian? Did we somehow break a local custom by asking? Did we have to be customers to even talk to her?

The entire day of frustration came to a boiling point of rage.

"Hey!" I yelled at the closed window, fist in the air, struggling to hold back my urge to pound on the glass. In that moment, all I wanted was to teach this woman a lesson in courtesy and respect, forgetting that I was about to throw both of those out the window myself. Suddenly, I felt Tracy's hand on my arm, pulling me away. When I turned around and looked at her, I saw tears running down her cheeks.

Tracy rarely cries, so I knew that her stomach must have been killing her. My anger was instantly replaced with concern. We had eight minutes left before everything closed. There was no time for me to give the magazine stand woman a profanity-laden lecture in humanity. So we moved on and left. Luckily, there was a convenience store not too far away, and we quickly found the medicine that Tracy needed.

Later that night, Tracy told me that she had cried not because of the stomach pain, but because of the way the woman had treated her. She felt indignant and hurt after being rudely shut down and rejected for no obvious reason. Hearing that somehow set off a sense of relief inside me. It was good that I hadn't known the true cause of her tears at the time, or I might have said or done something that I would later regret.

Our vacation got better in the days that followed. We met many friendly people, took romantic walks in Florence and Venice, and enjoyed the incredible food Italy had to offer. But we found ourselves talking to fewer people than we normally would, and we never asked anyone else for directions again.

How could one rude rejection by a person my wife and I had never met, and would never meet again, have such an impact on our emotions? The woman at the magazine stand hadn't caused any physical harm to Tracy, yet the rejection had felt worse than her excruciating stomach pain. As it happens, the reason for *that* turns out to be biological.

When humans feel physical pain, our brains release natural painkilling chemicals called opioids into our systems to lessen the pain and help us cope. Recently, researchers at the University of Michigan Medical School wondered if our brains would release opioids after social rejections as well, and they launched a study to find out.

In the study, they showed research participants' photos and fictitious profiles of hundreds of potential mates and then had them list which ones they'd be interested in dating. Then they used a brain scanner to monitor participants' brain activity while they were being told that the people they said they were interested in dating were *not* interested in them. The participants' brains, having experienced a social rejection, immediately started releasing opioids—just as

they would if a physical trauma had occurred. Even more interesting: participants had actually been told before the study
that the profiles—and the "rejections"—were fake. Incredibly, that didn't matter to their brains, which pumped out opioids regardless.

This is even more reason why simply saying "don't take it
personally" is useless advice for anyone feeling rejected. The
proverbial "slap in the face" we feel after being rejected isn't
so proverbial after all. No wonder Tracy and I felt so hurt by
the stranger in Italy that night. If she'd hurled a brick at us
through the magazine stand window, the effect would have
been more or less the same, at least to our brains.

## THE FEAR OF REJECTION

If the pain of rejection is actually a chemical experience in
your brain, it's no surprise that we develop a visceral fear
of rejection. It's the dread that stops you from even asking
a question in the first place—and sometimes covers you in
sweat as you get up the courage to make a request. Just remembering one experience of this kind of fear can make
people determined never to make themselves vulnerable to
it again.

Since rejection pain equals physical pain, at least to our
brains, it makes even more sense that people rank rejection
so high on their fear lists. After all, who isn't unnerved by
the idea of being slapped? But it turns out that many of our
fears—including our fear of rejection—actually have evolutionary roots as well.

Of all the research studies I read about the fear and pain

associated with rejection, some of the most interesting were the ones designed to show that phobias often have pragmatic, not to mention lifesaving, underpinnings. Numerous studies have shown that when it comes to avoiding objects or experiences that we instinctively judge to be harmful, our reaction times are much faster than they are when we're confronted by harmless objects or experiences. In other words, if you come across a deadly looking spider, you're going to clock a much faster sprint time running away from it than you could ever achieve if you were trying to outrun, say, a squirrel.

Researchers have concluded that mammals *evolved* an innate fear and alertness toward these harms in order to avoid and escape them faster. Fear, then, is required for our survival—or at least it was when we were out living on the savanna. Without the fear of snakes, there would be many more fatal snake bites; without the fear of enclosed spaces, more of us would be found, years later, stuck in drainpipes and crawl spaces.

The fear of rejection is no different. Back when we were hunting giant mastodons and living in caves, our survival depended on us sticking together and collaborating in groups. Being rejected or ostracized by our peers for whatever reason would leave us to face the wolves and the lions all by ourselves. In that situation, social rejection could equal death. It makes sense, then, that some of that instinct is still riding around in our DNA, even today—and that getting rejected can sometimes feel like a fate worse than death.

Finding all this out certainly made me feel better about my own intense fear of rejection—my instincts were just trying to keep me alive! But last time I checked, there were no mastodons roaming around downtown Austin. A social rejection wouldn't literally leave me out in the wild or force me to confront a beast all by myself. The fear of rejection may have saved many of our ancestors from getting tossed out of their social groups, but by and large it no longer makes sense in our modern lives. In fact, it's more baggage than a safety measure. If rejection fear were an organ, it would be an appendix instead of a heart. Yet its effect is much more damaging than the occasional appendicitis, because the consequence of not trying for new things due to the fear of rejection can't be fixed by a simple visit to the emergency room.

In my case, my fear of rejection had silently held me back, for more than a decade, from taking a step toward entrepreneurship. I can't help but wonder what this fear has done to millions of other lives. The list of regrets must be massive and heartbreaking. What exciting, interesting, and potentially life-changing ideas have people not pursued for fear of getting kicked out of the pack?

## 100 DAYS OF REJECTION: GIVE THE SAFETY ANNOUNCEMENT ON A PLANE

*"There are those who look at things the way they are, and ask why. . . . I dream things that never were, and ask why not."*

—ROBERT KENNEDY

As my 100 Days of Rejection went on, this quote had become my mantra. I used it to help override my instinct to back away from challenges. I was asking myself "Why not?" all the time, and I realized that there were often no logical reasons *not* to do—or at least try—most of the ideas that I had. One day I asked restaurant employees to sing me the "Happy Birthday" song although it wasn't actually my birthday. They did it! Another time I asked the local Humane Society if I could borrow or rent a dog for a day, promising I would do everything to provide the dog a fun day. They said no. Still another time I asked a Salvation Army bell ringer if I could ring the bell on his behalf. Not only did he say yes, we had a heck of a time doing it together.

But one of my "why not" requests really stood out. I was at the Austin airport, rushing from the parking lot to the terminal to catch my flight, when an idea popped into my head. I usually tune out when flight attendants make their preflight safety announcement, sending last-minute messages on my phone or getting settled in my seat. What if I took the matter into my own hands and asked the attendants on my flight to let me read the safety announcement on their behalf? I was flying Southwest, my favorite airline and one known for its quirky and customer-focused culture. If they let me do it, surely the passengers would pay closer attention. What was the harm in asking?

Still, I was a little nervous. While waiting to board the flight, I gathered myself, did some deep breathing, then approached a flight attendant. His name was Jeff.

"Do you think I can do the safety announcement for you guys?" I asked him, mentioning that I was a frequent flier.

For some reason, Jeff didn't seem too surprised by my request. He explained to me that by law, all passengers need to

be seated with their seat belts on while the safety announce-
ments are made. So unfortunately, since I was a passenger, I
couldn't make the announcement.

Then Jeff took me by surprise.

"But you can do the welcome thing if you can figure that
out," he said.

I stood there for a second, a bit shocked by the offer.
"Sure," I said. "I'll do the welcome thing. Awesome."

Jeff's offer was actually better than what I'd asked for, because it gave me the freedom to say whatever I wanted without having to read or memorize a scripted message. But now
I had a different problem. I would have to give a random,
spontaneous speech in front of 130 passengers. I could feel
the sweat forming on my palms as I went from feeling triumphant to terrified.

After Jeff gave the usual message about seat belts, emergency exits, and lavatories, he signaled to me to come to the
front. I went into the aisle and trudged toward him, row by
row. The walk seemed endless. I did everything I could to
block out thoughts of being booed or laughed at by other passengers, but those thoughts flooded me anyway. By the time
I made it to the front, I was an emotional mess with a pounding heart, churning stomach, and weak knees.

But then Jeff handed me the microphone and told me to
say whatever I wanted, as if he were 100 percent confident
that nothing could go wrong. I was a lot less confident; in
that moment, my fear did, in fact, seem deeply biological. I
could almost hear my DNA whispering to me, *Stop! You are
out of line. No one wants to hear you. You are making a fool of
yourself. People will reject you! Someone will think you are a ter-*

*rorist and tackle you! You are in danger!* I took the microphone from Jeff anyway, pushed the on button, and started talking.

"Hello, everyone, welcome on board!" I said, in my best flight attendant voice. Most people were looking at their phones, reading magazines, or chatting with one another. No one was paying attention.

"I am not a crew member," I said. Immediately, everyone raised their heads and looked at me. I felt hundreds of eyes on me. My nervousness moved closer to panic.

"I am just a fan of the company," I continued, speeding up my speech and trying not to let my voice shake. "I'm a customer like you. I just want to say they are always on time, they are always friendly, and they are always awesome! So if you are like me, give a round of applause to Southwest!"

Incredibly, everyone started clapping, just like I'd asked. As I walked back to my seat, another flight attendant pointed at me and said, "You get a free drink, man!" Another passenger blurted, "Wow . . . brave!"

*You have no idea*, I thought to myself as I sat back down in my seat, shaking and drenched in sweat. I'm sure fighting off lions with a stick ten thousand years ago was more difficult, but in the moment, this felt just as scary.

There were moments when I thought about quitting my 100 Days of Rejection, and my Southwest moment was one of them. I'd been preparing for a personal rejection from the flight attendant, but I'd received an acceptance instead, which in turn had opened up a much scarier possibility—a very public rejection by 130 people at the same time. Even though I managed my way through the ordeal, I felt pushed to the limit.

Before I learned about the biological roots of rejection, I thought I was fighting a monster through psychological warfare. But now I knew that I was fighting evolution, my own brain chemistry, and my DNA. The warfare wasn't just psychological—it was biological!

And that realization made me wonder: Did I really want to take on this fight? Was this a battle I was destined to lose? I began to wonder if this is what people meant when they said "ignorance is bliss."

But even as I worried that I didn't have what it took to deal with more rejection, I was able to gain strength by looking back on my earlier experiments. I could clearly see that not every rejection attempt had bathed me in sweat or triggered my internal terror, especially when I allowed myself to appreciate the humor in them. When I'd asked for a burger refill, I had left chuckling. When the grocery clerk refused to give me a tour of the warehouse, instead of running away, I'd started joking around with the guy. I hadn't walked out of those situations clutching my chest in pain—which made me think that maybe I had learned something else from my dealings with rejection without quite realizing it. Could humor be an effective way for me to neutralize rejection pain? To experiment, I staged another rejection attempt with laughter in mind.

## 100 DAYS OF REJECTION: A HAIR TRIM AT PETSMART

Driving past PetSmart one day, I remembered it was time to take my dog, Jumbo, in for some grooming. (It always seems like grooming time for golden retrievers; they are cute shedding machines.) As I pulled into the parking lot, an idea popped up in my head. What if I asked the dog groomers to cut *my* hair instead? The idea made me laugh—making it exactly the kind of rejection attempt that I wanted.

When I walked into the store's grooming area, four groomers were busily washing and trimming dogs. One of them stopped working and came over to greet me at the counter. After a few casual pleasantries, I asked how much it would cost for a hair trimming.

"What kind of dog?" she asked.

"How much would it cost to trim *my* hair?" I replied.

After a brief pause, she shook her head and said, "We don't do that." Then she burst out laughing.

"Then can you treat me like a German shepherd?" I asked. Then I remembered my Asian roots and appearance. "Actually, I am not German. Can you treat me like a Tibetan mastiff, or a chow chow or something?"

All four groomers started giggling.

"I'll behave. You can tell me to sit, and I'll sit and I won't bark," I said. I was on a roll.

"I'm sure you'll be the best client we have," the groomer joked back, laughing even harder.

I gave one last attempt before the rejection became final: "What about a manicure?" The groomers' laughter became almost uncontrollable.

Leaving PetSmart, I felt a sense of satisfaction. I didn't mind the no. In fact, I was feeling pretty good about myself because I figured I'd just made these groomers' day.

But why didn't I feel any pain or fear? How come my survival instinct hadn't kicked in, and the opioids hadn't started flowing? Why were they conspicuously silent this time?

I felt like I was onto something, and so I did some more research. It turns out that laughter has been linked to killing pain—literally.

There is a ton of anecdotal evidence that humor helps to reduce pain and stress—even among politicians, who are rarely known for their comedy. When heckled during a speech to the British Parliament, Ronald Reagan playfully replied, "Is there an echo in here?" Before going into surgery after his assassination attempt, he jokingly said to the surgeons: "I hope you are all Republicans." On the other side of the political spectrum, when a reporter pointedly asked John F. Kennedy how he felt about the Republican National Committee's adoption of a resolution that essentially called him a failure, he replied, "I assume it passed unanimously." Mahatma Gandhi even said: "If I had no sense of humor, I would long ago have committed suicide."

Researchers have even proved that humor—and laughter specifically—can actually mitigate pain. In 2011, Robin Dunbar, an evolutionary psychologist at Oxford University, ran an experiment in which he exposed participants to various degrees of pain by having them wear frozen wine-cooling sleeves on their arms or keep their legs bent ninety degrees while leaning against a wall, as if they were sitting on an imaginary chair. To determine their normal pain threshold, Dunbar measured how long participants could resist the pain before admitting that they couldn't take it anymore.

Then he subjected participants to the same pain again,

but this time while showing them a variety of videos, from comedies such as *The Simpsons* and *South Park*, to neutral videos featuring pet training and golf, to documentaries meant to evoke good feelings, such as *Planet Earth*. He found that participants' pain thresholds significantly increased only when they watched the comedies—and specifically when they laughed. On the other hand, neutral and feeling-good films made no difference. In another words, laughter reduced their pain and stress.

Dunbar believes that the power of laughter even has evolutionary roots. "Dr. Dunbar thinks laughter may have been favored by evolution because it helped bring human groups together, the way other activities like dancing and singing do," wrote reporter James Gorman in the *New York Times*. Laughing, dancing, and singing all produce endorphins—a different kind of opioid that not only fights pain but also makes us feel good. Laughing can be like receiving a double shot of natural painkillers from our brain.

So that explained why I didn't feel much pain during the rejection attempts that left me laughing. The fear and pain that might have been generated by the experience were suppressed by endorphins because I was amusing myself simultaneously. In the case of my PetSmart adventure, I left feeling better about myself after being rejected.

In my search for the right stone to hurl at Goliath, I felt like I had stumbled on a good one. Laughter was not only good for me, but it quickly became one of my most effective weapons—my own evolution-based, biological weapon—for fighting off rejection pain and for helping me to stay calm and think on my feet.

Of course, humor has its limitations. Silliness isn't appropriate in every real-life situation, and I knew I wouldn't be able to rely on humor to help me through every rejection attempt—especially when the stakes are high and the outcomes have real significance. Also, endorphins address only the results of rejection—the pain. They don't address the fear and the anticipation of rejection, which are the roots of rejection's destructive power. But it also provoked another question: If something can't hurt me, then why should it scare me? It turned out it's this question that proved to be pivotal in my fight with rejection.

In the movie *The Wizard of Oz*, Dorothy, the Scarecrow, the Tin Man, and the Lion went on an arduous journey to the Emerald City. They wanted to meet the "great and powerful" Wizard of Oz, who they hope will grant their wishes to return home, get a brain, receive a heart, and gain courage. When they visited the Wizard, they walked through a long creepy hallway, fighting the urge to run away. When they finally arrived in the room, they saw the Wizard as a menacing green-looking bald monster floating over a throne surrounded by fire, smoke, and steam. He spoke in a terrifying and threatening tone. He demanded that they set out on a mission and was so pushy and mean that he scared them senseless—so literally that the Lion actually lost consciousness.

After they finished the mission given by the Wizard, they returned to the Emerald City. As the Wizard carried on with his terrifying display, Dorothy's little dog, Toto, trotted over to a large curtain in the corner of the room. He tugged it down, suddenly revealing the real Wizard. He was a normal-looking gray-haired man operating an audio and visual machine to create the terrifying image in order to scare his visitors.

In reality, there was nothing frightening about this man—what became larger than life were the rumors, the mysteries, and the façade that the Wizard had constructed around himself. But what made it real was the way everyone else reacted to it.

My journey to meet and study rejection felt like Dorothy's journey to the Emerald City. On that Southwest flight, I experienced the fear of public rejection in full force. I felt as though I was in that room meeting the terrifying and dangerous Wizard. But whenever I injected humor into my rejection attempts, I felt like I was peering behind the curtain to see the real Wizard, who was harmless and even funny. I was seeing rejection through a completely different lens.

Most of the time, when you really look at it, rejection is like the Wizard of Oz. We might be terrified of rejection when we're asking for a raise, a date, an investment, or the approval we crave. We feel the word *no* comes at us with a loud voice, fire, and smoke. We feel it would really hurt us. But in reality, it is almost never that bad. Even if we don't get what we ask for, we haven't lost anything. It is rarely the case that our lives are in danger.

In my own life, I had never taken the time to get behind the curtain and see what rejection—my own "Wizard of Oz"—really was, until then.

Now I had to ask myself: *What is this thing that I've been fighting all my life? What exactly is rejection?*

# CHAPTER 5

# RETHINKING REJECTION

**W**HEN I BEGAN MY REJECTION JOURNEY, I DESPER-
ately wanted to slay my Goliath. Within a few weeks
of searching for rejection, I could feel myself getting better
at it. I hit a rejection groove, with each rejection seeming to
get easier. One day I brought my own pork chop to a BBQ
restaurant and asked to grill my own food. Another day I
challenged a stranger to a staring contest. Neither experience left me sweating.

The further I got in my journey, the more I wanted to
study and understand rejection so that I could apply what I
was learning to the rest of my life. So I started to increase the
"fear factor" of my rejection attempts, making them more
like real-life scenarios to see what I could learn. One of those
rejection attempts in particular got the job done—literally.

## 100 DAYS OF REJECTION: FINDING A JOB IN ONE DAY

My blog made it easy for people to get in touch with me, and I was receiving dozens of fan e-mails per day. It was the beginning of 2013, the economy was still sluggish, and there was a lot of competition for seemingly every available job. Not surprisingly, a lot of people wrote to me to express both their frustration and their fear of rejection when it comes to searching for work. So I decided to do a job-related rejection attempt to see if I could learn something about how to make the job search easier. Moreover, by that time it had been years since I last looked for a job. I wanted to experience a job-search rejection firsthand so that I could help others with theirs.

I didn't go the networking-application-interview route. Instead, I decided to simply show up at random office buildings with my résumé in hand and ask for a one-day job. The request felt a little bit awkward—who asks for a job lasting only one day? But my curiosity about what would happen far outweighed my nervousness.

When you are not afraid of rejection and it feels like you have nothing to lose, amazing things can happen.

In my first two stops, I was quickly turned away by stern-faced office managers. One of them even gave me a lecture on how I shouldn't just drop in and needed to follow the formal application process. Undeterred, I walked into a third office building for one last try before calling it a day.

The office manager who greeted me had a smile that would put anyone, including potential job seekers, at ease.

Her name was Jennifer Carrier. After hearing my request, she didn't kick me out. In fact, she wanted to know more about why I was asking for a job in the first place. I explained that as an entrepreneur I hadn't looked for a job for a while, so I wanted to see if I could do it by dropping by an office. Then I did my best to convince her that I would be an excellent employee and would give my best effort to whatever job she would give me, whether it was online marketing—my specialty back at the Fortune 500 company I'd quit—or manual labor. In the end, I asked her to hire me as her personal assistant for one day. After some consideration, she gave me a provisional yes, adding that she would have to consult with her boss before it was official.

A few days later, Jennifer called. She presented me with an "offer" to work at her company for one day as an assistant office manager. The company was BigCommerce, an Austin-based technology firm that creates websites for small businesses. I would be helping Jennifer with her daily duties, such as greeting visitors, solving logistical issues for the office and its employees, and ordering lunch.

I took the offer and, a few days later, reported for duty. I spent the morning working with Jennifer. During an afternoon company meeting, I made another rejection attempt, asking the company's managers to put my face on their website. Incredibly, a day later, my picture made its appearance.

## REJECTION IS HUMAN

Without the help of a recruiter or an agency, without filling out online application forms, without doing any sit-down interviews or handing over my references, I had found a job. And it had taken me only three tries. Sure, I wasn't asking BigCommerce to make a long-term investment in me; getting a full-time job with a good salary and benefits is harder than volunteering somewhere for a day. But I felt like I had learned something about how to interact with prospective employers that I hadn't known before.

It would be naive to give full credit to my strategy, to my persistence, or to any persuasive abilities I might possess; outside factors had played an equally if not more important role in the outcome. Namely, Jennifer, the office manager for BigCommerce, said yes to me, while most office managers wouldn't. After getting to know Jennifer, I learned that she was known for her welcoming spirit, sense of humor, and love of adventure. When I interviewed her later to find out why she'd said yes, she told me that having a well-spoken man with a good résumé stop by the office looking for a one-day job had piqued her curiosity. But as we talked more, I realized that it was about much more than that.

Jennifer grew up in Massachusetts. Her father was a salesman who taught her to be inquisitive about people's intentions and not to dismiss their requests. Her mom, who was from the South, taught her the value of hospitality. Being rather shy and quiet in high school, Jennifer was sent to modeling school for a year by her father. There, she learned

that a smile and a positive attitude could be just as important to a person's appearance as his or her natural looks. In
college, she worked in restaurants as a waitress to put herself
through school. Being a waitress taught her to never say no
to a customer's request without first trying to find a solution.

All these experiences and perspectives made Jennifer
who she was. And all of them were in play on the day that I
knocked on her office door and asked for a job.

Jennifer was certainly the exception rather than norm,
and the fact that I ran into someone like her on my third try,
rather than the tenth or fifteenth, was a stroke of luck. Had
I not run into Jennifer, I would have ended my rejection attempt with a no. There would have been no one-day job and
no opportunity to share my learning with my viewers. On
the other hand, I could have been even luckier and gotten
Jennifer on my first try. In that case, I would have stopped
after getting the first yes and possibly come to the misguided
conclusion that most office managers welcomed strangers
looking for jobs. I was grateful for the perspective that experiencing both possible outcomes had given me.

Through this experiment, I observed a very important
fact: people could react to the same request very differently,
and it said nothing about me. I was the same person posing the same question—"Can I work here for one day?"—to
three different people at three different offices. Their responses reflected their own attitudes, sense of curiosity, and
risk tolerance—which varied quite a bit among them.

A lot of people—including my pre-rejection experiment
self—might lose confidence in themselves after getting a
few rejections. Every time they ask for what they want, they

feel that the "universe" is making a unanimous judgment on their merits. But Jennifer helped me see that this couldn't be true. The "universe" is made up of people with diverse and often polar-opposite personalities, incentives, and backgrounds. Their reactions to a certain request reveal much more about them than about the request itself.

I started to realize that rejection is a human interaction, with at least two parties involved in every decision. When we forget this—and see the people who say yes or no to us as faceless machines—every rejection can feel like an indictment, and every acceptance like a validation. But that's just not the case.

## REJECTION IS AN OPINION

This job-seeking experience also sparked another paradigm shift. From that point on, rejection seemed less like "the truth" and more like an opinion. Other people were simply processing my requests, then giving me their opinions. That opinion could be based on their mood, their needs and circumstances at that moment, or their knowledge, experience, education, culture, and upbringing over a lifetime. Whatever was guiding them at the time I entered their lives, these forces were usually much stronger than my presentation, my personality, or my request itself.

People often use the phrase "everyone is entitled to their own opinion." In fact, everyone has opinions—sometimes very strong ones that they can't wait to share. Ranging from politics to people and from food preferences to music taste, our opinions couldn't be more diverse. If I accepted every opinion equally and used it to judge the merit of something, not only would I change my mind constantly but I would probably eventually lose it.

Throughout history, many great ideas that ultimately propelled humanity forward were initially met with vocal, violent, and even gruesome rejection by society at large. They include the movements led by Socrates, Galileo, Joan of Arc, Mahatma Gandhi, Nelson Mandela, and Martin Luther King Jr. Even the foundation of Christianity was formed by the rejection of Jesus by his own people.

Moreover, people's opinions change over time, across regions, and are heavily influenced by social, political, and environmental factors that are outside any one person's control. People are susceptible to the societal pressures that encourage (or demand) that they behave in a certain way.

Yale social psychologist Stanley Milgram designed one of the most famous, if not notorious, experiments, called the Milgram Shock Experiment, to demonstrate just how influenced people can be by the presence of an authority figure. In the experiment, an actor who wore an authoritative-looking lab coat ordered research participants to give out a fake electric shock to another actor in the adjacent room, pretending to be a fellow research participant. Not knowing the shock was fake and the experiment was staged, the participant would follow the order and deliver shocks, often to the maximum and life-threatening level. The experiment was so profound because it showed that people would say yes in the name of following orders from authorities.

Outside influences have an enormous impact on the way people see a situation—and those influences can change over time. The way someone feels about me, or about a request I'm making, can be impacted by factors that have nothing to do with me. If people's opinions and behaviors can change so drastically based on so many different factors, why should I take everything about a rejection so personally? This simple but profound realization helped me to start taking the emotion out of rejection—and to look with new eyes at the decisions people make.

I decided that I wanted to use 100 Days of Rejection as an experiment to test out whether it was possible for an idea to be deemed universally good or bad. I wanted to create a rejection attempt where I offered people something that I would never accept myself, and that I was sure no other person would ever accept. Would it be possible that someone else would have such a different opinion that the person might find it acceptable?

Coming up with a rejection idea along these lines was harder than it sounds. So I called someone renowned for his ability to design wacky social experiments—Dan Ariely, a professor of behavioral economics at Duke University. His bestselling books, *Predictably Irrational* and *The Honest Truth About Dishonesty*, are filled with such experiments. I'd taken one of Dan's classes when I was a graduate student and found him to be one of the funniest and most thoughtful people I'd ever encountered. Behavioral economics is about the study of psychological, social, and emotional influences on people's decision making. If I wanted to run a social experiment related to human behavior, Dan was the first person I'd call for advice.

So I called him up. I told him about the amazing and

wild rejection journey I'd been on. Then I asked if he had any ideas about how to come up with a rejection attempt that nobody would ever say yes to.

Dan not only loved my story, but also quickly started churning out wacky ideas for me to try. One of his ideas immediately struck me as brilliant, and I decided to give it a go.

## 100 DAYS OF REJECTION: GIVING APPLES TO STRANGERS

From the book of Genesis to the fairy tale of Snow White, from the Halloween trick-or-trick urban legend about razors-in-apples to every responsible mom's advice, taking an apple from a stranger has always been a very bad idea.

So I bought some apples from a store, then offered them to strangers in a parking lot. I named my blog entry "Evil Queen and the Six Snow Whites." I would be the evil queen giving away apples. And no way any "Snow Whites" would bite. Right?

To find out, I headed to the parking lot of my local Target, positioned myself on the sidewalk near the exit doors, and started offering apples to shoppers. Not surprisingly, most people turned me down right away. One woman even had a conversation with me about why she was so scared by an offer like this, citing food safety and emotional concerns. She looked traumatized when she recalled to me a restaurant experience where someone had tampered with her food.

However, one well-dressed woman really blew my mind. When I offered her an apple, she said: "OK, thanks!" She took the apple and walked away like nothing strange had happened. A couple of steps later, she bit into it.

I almost fell to the ground as if I'd bitten a poisonous apple myself. How could anyone just eat food from a stranger without a second thought?

I regret not chasing after her and asking why she took the apple. But whatever the reason, I knew her decision had to be based on a judgment that she made of me. She had sized up the stranger with the bag of apples and the crazy offer, and formed the opinion that accepting the apple would be OK. Maybe there were factors that I couldn't know about that made my offering seem more appealing—she might have missed a meal, or been trying to eat more fruit, or maybe she just thought I looked too friendly to have tampered with the food.

If a bad idea like eating unwrapped food from a stranger isn't universally rejected, do universally rejected ideas even exist? And if not, maybe that means that the only reason you get rejected from things is because you haven't met the right person to say it yet.

## REJECTION HAS A NUMBER

One of my favorite bits of movie dialogue is from *Money Never Sleeps*, the sequel to the classic film *Wall Street*, when the young hero, Jacob Moore, confronts the corporate villain, Bretton James, on his shady business ethics and voracious appetite for money.

JACOB: "What's your number?"

BRETTON: "Excuse me?"

JACOB: "The amount of money you would need to be able

to walk away from it all and just live happily ever after. See, I find that everyone has a number and it's usually an exact number, so what is yours?"

BRETTON, WITH A RUTHLESS SMILE, REPLIES: "More."

Through my rejection experiments, I began to realize that I could often get a yes simply by talking to enough people. Obviously, not every rejection attempt would ultimately yield a yes, especially some of the wackier ones. But I was surprised by how many times my persistence paid off—like it had with the apple experiment, and with my attempt to land a one-day-only office job. It made me wonder: Do rejections also have a "number"? If you ask enough people for something enough times, will you eventually find someone to say yes?

When it comes to persistence, one group of people who are constantly coming up against rejection are people who work in creative fields. EJ, a fiction author, e-mailed me with a rejection challenge:

"I'm an author and I would love to work with you on the next Rejection Therapy video," she wrote. "I see writers get rejected every day; most writers carry tons of rejections and never get accepted by these big intimidating publishing houses. I think it would send quite a message, and probably go viral in the extremely large literary community, to walk up to the publishers, in their building and onto their executive floor, hand these guys a manuscript, and ask them, 'Can you publish my book?'"

While that experiment never came to fruition, EJ's letter

did make me think more about the life of a writer. I wondered how many times famous authors had been rejected by publishers before one of them finally accepted their first book.

When I actually looked into it, the numbers were astonishing:

- *Lord of the Flies* by William Golding: 20
- *The Diary of a Young Girl* by Anne Frank: 15
- *Carrie* by Stephen King: 30
- *Zen and the Art of Motorcycle Maintenance* by Robert M. Pirsig: 121 (a record in the *Guinness Book of World Records*)
- *Dubliners* by James Joyce: 22
- *The Help* by Kathryn Stockett: 60
- *Harry Potter and the Philosopher's Stone* by J. K. Rowling: 12
- *The Cuckoo's Calling* (J. K. Rowling using the pseudonym Robert Galbraith): at least one confirmed, allegedly many more

It wasn't just the numbers, either; some of the feedback these authors received from the rejecting publishers was extremely harsh:

> "The girl doesn't, it seems to me, have a special perception or feeling which could lift that book above the 'curiosity' level."—on Anne Frank: *The Diary of a Young Girl*

> "An absurd and uninteresting fantasy which was rubbish and dull."—on *Lord of the Flies*

"We are not interested in science fiction which deals
with negative utopias. They do not sell."—*on Carrie*

"It's far too long for children"—*on Harry Potter and the
Philosopher's Stone*

J. K. Rowling's rejections are especially fascinating. In
1995, she submitted her first Harry Potter manuscript to
twelve British publishers and was rejected by all of them.
Then the head of one publisher, Bloomsbury, handed the
manuscript to her granddaughter, who couldn't put it down
until she finished reading the entire thing. Bloomsbury finally gave Harry Potter the green light a year later. Had the
little girl not loved the story, Harry Potter might have landed
in the shredder, and his epic battle with You-Know-Who
would have never happened.

More than a decade later, *Harry Potter* sold over 100 million copies and became one of the top ten bestselling books
in history. J. K. Rowling sent out the manuscript of her new
book, *The Cuckoo's Calling*, to publishers under a pseudonym
because she wanted her work to stand on its own merit rather
than on her fame. The editor who read and rejected the book,
which would also become a bestseller, had said it was "quiet"
and "didn't stand out."

All these rejections have now become jokes and inspirational tales because of how successful the books and authors
went on to be. But I suspect that every no these authors received discouraged—maybe even devastated—them. It's
hard not to wonder how many would-be masterpieces have
never seen the light of day because the creators were so dis-

couraged by the rejections and negative opinions and stopped trying.

All these authors—many of whom are now considered to be the greatest talents of their days—had to push beyond dozens of rejections until they found the right person who agreed to publish their work. It's as if becoming a master of a craft requires not just great skills, but also the ability to weather rejections to get to an acceptance—not to mention an unfailing belief in themselves and their own work.

No matter how good or bad the work is, there is no mathematical way for everyone in the world to accept or reject it. But if acceptance is the only thing a person strives for, all she or he needs to do is to talk to enough people. Odds are that someone will eventually say yes.

Of course, not all acceptances are created equal. Not every book idea will lead to a giant bestselling franchise the way that J. K. Rowling's did; there is good and bad, after all. However, thinking about all those authors who had believed so much in their work that they kept trying to find a publisher after so many painful rejections made me realize how important it was to believe in what I was doing. Rejection is human, is an opinion, and has a number. If I viewed other people's opinions as the main judgment of merit—which is what I was doing when I took every rejection to heart—then my life would be a miserable mess. I'd be basing my self-worth, and even the course of my life, on the whims and judgments of other people.

All these years, rejection had scared me like Goliath. It stopped me from pursuing my dreams for over a decade. It sometimes stopped me from reaching out or even saying "hi" to others for fear of rejection and judgment. But now that I was studying Goliath, and seeing him with new eyes, it felt as if I might have him cornered. Without the fog of pain and fear, rejection wasn't the Goliath that I'd thought it was. Instead, it was more like the Wizard of Oz. It didn't have to be my enemy—if I didn't let it scare me to death.

## LESSONS

1. Rejection Is Human: Rejection is a human interaction with two sides. It often says more about the rejector than the rejectee, and should never be used as the universal truth and sole judgment of merit.

2. Rejection Is an Opinion: Rejection is an opinion of the rejector. It is heavily influenced by historical context, cultural differences, and psychological factors. There is no universal rejection or acceptance.

3. Rejection Has a Number: Every rejection has a number. If the rejectee goes through enough rejections, a no could turn into a yes.

CHAPTER 6

# TAKING A NO

**A**T ABOUT THE HALFWAY POINT OF MY 100 DAYS, MY fear of rejection was transforming into something more like curiosity. This shift in perspective opened the door for me to start experimenting with rejection even more. I wanted to poke and study rejection from different sides. And the first thing I wanted to explore was finding out what could happen *after* I received a no.

In the past, I'd always figured that the best way to minimize the pain of rejection was to get it over with as soon as possible—sort of like ripping a bandage off in one motion versus peeling it off slowly and prolonging the agony. In most cases, I would run away—sometimes literally—after hearing a no, ending the conversation as quickly as possible.

Now, I wanted to see what would happen if instead of fleeing the scene of a rejection, I would stick around to find out what would happen next. Little did I know how much I would learn by simply not running away.

## ASK "WHY" BEFORE GOOD-BYE
### 100 DAYS OF REJECTION: PLANTING A FLOWER IN SOMEONE'S YARD

After I'd posted the video of playing soccer in Scott the football fan's backyard, people started asking me to knock on more strangers' doors for various things—everything from borrowing a cup of sugar to asking to spend the night in their house. Amid all the creative suggestions, one in particular caught my eye: asking permission to plant a flower in someone's yard. I loved the idea because (1) it was strange enough to almost guarantee a no and (2) if I did happen to get a yes, I'd be contributing to the beauty of someone's landscaping.

After buying a peach-colored, ready-to-plant Double Delight rosebush, I started driving around Austin looking for a good house to approach. The last time I found myself driving around looking for a door to knock on, I was extremely nervous. But I'd become a rejection veteran by this time. I picked a house, walked up to the door, and just knocked. The life-and-death feeling I had back when I'd approached Scott's house was almost nonexistent now.

This time, a white-haired man answered the door. He immediately eyed the rosebush in my hands—it was hard to miss. He probably assumed I was a salesman, because he didn't look eager for conversation. Then I explained that I wanted to plant the rosebush in his yard, free of charge. He raised an eyebrow and gave a slight smile.

"OK, that's more interesting than I thought," he admitted, almost sheepishly. "Thank you, but no."

This was the moment—my chance to see what happens after a no. As he was about to close the door, I said, "No problem. But may I ask why?"

"Well, I don't like flowers in my yard," he explained. "My dog would dig them up and destroy them. I appreciate you doing this, but you've got the wrong guy."

He looked at the rosebush again. "I like you giving out these flowers," he said. "If you go across the street and ask Lauren, she might want it. She loves flowers."

This was an unexpected turn of events. I said "thank you" and went across the street. Armed with this new information, and feeling a surge of both confidence and excitement, I ventured toward Lauren's house. I caught her and her husband just as they were about to leave. After hearing my offer and conferring with her husband, she agreed to let me plant the Double Delight in their yard.

"I love peach roses," Lauren gushed, genuinely thrilled at the new addition to her yard.

The rosebush that I planted, with its straight stem and two angled branches, resembled the letter Y. It was almost a literal reminder of the power of asking "why" after getting rejected. By engaging in conversation with the man, I learned two very valuable things:

1. The man rejected me not because he didn't trust me or thought I was weird. He appreciated my offer, but it didn't fit his situation.

2. He gave me a lead to another person who he knew might be much more open to my gift.

In my first-ever rejection attempt, I had asked my office building's security guard if I could borrow $100. After saying "No," he'd asked me a question: "Why?" Feeling scared and embarrassed, I bolted without explaining myself. But ever since then I hadn't been able to get his response out of my head.

When Scott, the avid Cowboys fan, let me play soccer in his backyard, I'd asked him why he agreed to my request. He said it was so "off the wall" that he couldn't turn me down. Learning the reason he'd felt compelled to say yes gave me insight into Scott and his decision. But it happened only because of the word *why*.

Asking the white-haired man why he didn't want a rosebush in his yard had produced a different kind of result: an explanation *and* a referral. He might have turned me down, but he had given me a lead that converted into a yes.

Asking why tended to clear up any misunderstanding on my part about the other person's motivations. In the past, when I was rejected, I had automatically assumed that I'd done something wrong. But by spending a little more time with the man who initially turned me down, I'd discovered that what I was offering simply didn't fit his situation. There was nothing personal about it; he didn't want a rosebush, not just from me but from anybody. And I didn't think he was giving me a fake reason just to get me off his porch; otherwise, he wouldn't have recommended that I talk to his flower-loving neighbor.

There is a reason behind every decision that people make, whether it's logical and well thought out or emotional and spur of the moment. Knowing the reason behind a rejection can help dissipate, or even dissolve, any of the pain one might feel otherwise. Many of the people who rejected me did so not because of the merit of my request, or because of anything about me, but for a completely different reason—sometimes one that was easily addressable. Once I understood that, I realized I was able to cope with the rejection much more easily. I even learned to use rejections as learning experiences to make my requests even better the next time.

There's only an upside to asking "why." After all, you have been rejected already. And the insight you might glean from the response you get could prove valuable. Indeed, asking "why" can even be a tool for turning a rejection into an acceptance.

## RETREAT, DON'T RUN
### 100 DAYS OF REJECTION: MCDONALD'S CHALLENGE
### (GETTING AFTERNOON MCGRIDDLES)

As the 100 Days project went on, I started getting more suggestions from people daring me to try all kinds of things. One day, a follower dared me to march into a local McDonald's in the middle of the afternoon and ask them to make me a McGriddles sandwich, a breakfast item that they only offer in the morning. He felt confident that I would be "100%

rejected" because it is "impossible" for McDonald's to make breakfast items after 12 P.M.

It was 2 P.M. when I asked the McDonald's clerk for a Mc-Griddles sandwich. As expected, I got a very quick no. After I asked her why, she explained that they'd already cleaned the machine that makes the eggs and the sausage. So I switched tactics.

"Do you have something *like* a McGriddles?" I asked. That piqued the clerk's interest. She said she could make me a "plain McGriddles"—which turned out to be a honey roasted griddle cake with cheese on it. I went for it. Taking my sandwich to a table, I turned my iPhone around to record myself and claim victory over the fan's "impossible" challenge. The sandwich wasn't as good without the eggs and the sausage. But I ate the whole thing anyway, and it was really not bad.

The McDonald's challenge started out as something a bit silly, but it ended up coughing up another important lesson. I had tried a negotiation tactic that would turn out to be another important weapon in my arsenal. Instead of setting my goals on only the specific thing that I'd gone in asking for, I reassessed my original request and asked for something less—in this case, something "like a McGriddles." The clerk recognized my concession and met me halfway by offering a solution.

In military warfare, there is a crucial distinction between a retreat and a rout. Retreats are usually temporary. Troops retreat in order to regroup, consolidate their forces, or shift to a better tactical position. A rout, on the other hand, is a total collapse of troops' fighting ability and morale. In a rout, the losing troops often drop their weapons and run for their lives. The defenseless fleeing soldiers have their backs turned to the enemy, making them vulnerable targets. Many times it is during routs that the most casualties have occurred.

For people who are afraid of or anxious about rejection, asking for things can feel like a mini-battlefield. When you are already so uncomfortable making the request, it can be hard to judge whether you should keep going or get the hell out of there after a no. I had found (1) that if I kept insisting on getting what I wanted regardless of what the other person said, the other person would get annoyed and shut me down cold, and (2) that if I turned and fled, I would create a rout of my own making. In both situations, I would leave without getting what I wanted or needed, and I would leave myself vulnerable not just to the judgment of others but to the assumptions and to the demoralizing stories that I would tell myself about the encounter. The biggest casualty in those "battles" was not the rejection but my resulting loss of confidence.

The McGriddles moment taught me that there was a powerful third way—retreating, reassessing, and trying a new approach. If I could adjust my request and approach the "ask" from a different angle, something interesting and unexpected might happen—and it often did. For one rejection attempt, I tried to get a free room at a luxury hotel and was turned down flat. But after retreating to a lesser request, I wound up getting a tour of one of the hotel's rooms and was allowed to take a nap on one of the hotel's famously comfortable beds. During another rejection attempt, I walked into a local fire station and asked if I could slide down their fire pole. As it happened, the building had only one story, and there was no fire pole. So I again retreated to a lesser request—and soon found myself on a tour of the fire station, with the firefighter on duty as my personal tour guide. He even offered to let me ride on their fire truck.

In his classic book on psychology and communication, *Influence*, Robert Cialdini explains the effectiveness of making a concession and retreating to a lesser request after an initial rejection. He argues that because most people don't want to feel like jerks, they are much less likely to say no the second time to the requester after the requester makes a concession. That's why successful negotiations that result in win-win situations are usually the results of give-and-take rather than both parties digging in and refusing to compromise.

Asking why can open up a whole new channel of understanding and possibility between a requester and a requestee. But so can retreating to ask, "If you can't do this, can you do something else?" In asking these questions again and again, it became obvious to me that there is often a lot more room to maneuver around a no than I'd ever realized. Every no is actually surrounded by a whole bunch of interesting but invisible yeses that it was up to me to uncover.

If you get turned down for a job, one option is to flee—but another option is to ask for recommendations for other positions based on your qualifications. If someone shoots down your sales pitch, you could ask for a referral to another department or client. By having a position to retreat to—and keeping an open mind—you can often avoid being routed by rejection.

## COLLABORATE, DON'T CONTEND

### 100 DAYS OF REJECTION: INVENT MY OWN ICE CREAM FLAVOR

When I was a kid in China, I had a lot of big dreams. One of them was to dig a hole through the earth from China to America. At age six, I actually started digging that hole on the side of the street I grew up on. But after two days—and about three feet of soil—someone told my mom. That was the end of my adventure, and my trip to America was delayed by another decade.

Another childhood dream of mine was to invent my own flavor of ice cream—but I'd never tried to turn this dream into a reality. Now that I was deep into my rejection journey and far savvier about how to maneuver through a no to land somewhere interesting, it felt like the right time to try.

After giving my flavor ideas some thought, I headed to Amy's Ice Cream, a local landmark shop famous for its great ice cream—as well as for the flashy dancelike moves that its clerks do while preparing ice cream and toppings for customers. Thankfully, this time my mom wasn't there to stop me.

After walking into the shop, I asked the store clerk to make me ice cream with a flavor I dubbed "Thai Torture." I described the flavor as a combination of dried pepper, jalapeño, and ghost chili—the spiciest ingredients I could imagine. I once ordered food at a Thai restaurant with a spicy rating of 51 out of 50. But the next two days were nothing but internal torture. Thai Torture was a flavor I was sure nobody would ever want—and one that no ice cream clerk would ever make for me.

Not surprisingly, the clerk said no and directed my attention toward the store's ice cream flavor menu. But instead of walking away—or settling for vanilla—I started asking more questions. When I asked if they had any spicy flavors, the clerk told me that they actually sold a few during the summer (this was wintertime), including a couple of jalapeño flavors and another called "chocolate wasabi." He went into the freezer to search for them but couldn't find any. But he said that if I brought in my own flavoring, he would gladly customize the ice cream for me.

In the end, the clerk gave me some samples of Amy's wacky bacon-and-mint-flavored ice cream, and I loved it. It surely tasted better than Thai Torture would have.


Looking back, the clerk had literally come out from behind the counter and over to my side so that we could share a common view of the situation. It wasn't a you-vs.-me zero-sum game, but an us-vs.-them problem-solving game. Solving the problem was a win for both of us. Plus, he had given me an opening to create my own flavor if I met him halfway by bringing in my own ingredients.

When I feared rejection, it felt natural to view the people who hold the power to grant me a yes or a no as adversaries. But after I shifted that thinking and started viewing them as *collaborators*, I suddenly found myself in whole new territory. I didn't approach the Amy's Ice Cream clerk with any negative feelings, and that even-keeled mental approach enabled me to maintain positivity and respect. By asking him questions about the problem at hand, I turned him into a collaborator, which prompted him to put on his customer service hat and help me toward my goals. And—as I'd already experienced again and again—the end results were better than what I asked for.

On the flip side, the opposite of collaboration—argument—is a magnet for rejection. And nothing drove this point home for me more than the experience I had with a documentary film crew that drove from Los Angeles to Austin to make a short piece about my rejection journey. They were particularly intrigued by how I managed to get so many yeses with such crazy requests. At the time, I was trying to understand this myself, so I agreed to take them with me on a rejection excursion.

Austin, whose official nickname is "Live Music Capital of the World," is filled with independent music studios. The employees of these studios are usually part-time musicians themselves. The idea was to show up at one of these studios and ask one of its employees to perform his or her favorite music piece for us.

Curious to see what would happen if someone else made the request, we had Ethan, one of the documentary team's crew members, try it out. He approached the employee manning the front desk and asked him if he could show us the studio and perform some music. The guy behind the desk said no. He told us he was working and looked a little annoyed.

Ethan started arguing, telling the employee that it was his job to accommodate potential customers' requests. The employee in turn argued that the studio had a policy against employees or customers using its instruments without permission or pay. The two of them went back and forth, their voices rising. Our "rejection request" was quickly degenerating into a verbal fight about rules and responsibilities.

I knew from experience that this would not end well, so I stepped in. "We know it's an unusual request and would be perfectly fine if you say no," I said. "But we would really appreciate it if you say yes. We simply want to hear you play some drums for us in this studio."

The employee looked at me, then looked toward the ceiling, and then started nodding his head. "OK," he said. And just like that, he led us into the studio's best drum room and started playing his favorite beat.

The documentary crew's jaws dropped. Not only were they able to film a rejection attempt and drum performance, but they saw a rejection turned into acceptance in front of their eyes. After we thanked the employee and left the studio, the crew asked me what type of voodoo spell I'd put on that guy to have him say yes to me just a few seconds after he had said no to Ethan.

Given all that I'd learned, it actually made sense. Arguing with a person who turns you down is probably the least effective way to change the individual's response. In fact, it's almost a sure way to get a rejection, because arguing always turns potential collaborators into enemies. I'd approached the music studio employee as a collaborator, and that switch in approach had changed his mind. By making it clear that he had the freedom to say no, I got to the yes we were looking for.

## SWITCH UP, DON'T GIVE UP

To quit or not to quit? That's a question that lingers in the mind of almost everyone who has failed at something. On one side, self-help gurus and motivational speakers preach Winston Churchill's quote "Never give in, never give in, never, never, never—in nothing, great or small, large or petty—never give in" or Vince Lombardi's quote "Winners never quit and quitters never win." On the other side, modern entrepreneurs preach quick pivoting on unattainable ideas. Their motto is "fail fast, fail often." Bestselling authors and economists Steven Levitt and Stephen Dubner even dedicated an entire chapter to the "Upside of Quitting" in their book *Think Like a Freak*.

When it comes to rejection, there is also merit for both arguments. In my 100 Days of Rejection, sometimes no matter what approaches or tactics I tried, a no remained a no. In these cases, continuing to make the same request over and over again under the same conditions, with the same person, in the hope that my persistence would somehow change the outcome almost always proved counterproductive and impractical.

But instead of quitting, I found that stepping back and trying again under different circumstances could yield a different result. I call it "switch up." In my efforts to find a one-day job, it took three different companies to get to yes. When I tried to plant flowers in someone's yard, the second person, Lauren, gave me the green light. Approaching a different person, rather than continuously trying to convince the same person again and again, regardless of his needs and preferences, was much more productive.

Another way to "switch up" is to change environments.

Stephon Marbury has been a big-time sports star ever since he was little. Born and raised in Brooklyn, he quickly earned the nickname "Starbury" due to his basketball talent and was widely viewed as the next great NBA point guard. In high school, he received the "Mr. New York Basketball" award and was named a McDonald's All-American—two very prestigious titles. He was also featured in a book and on the cover of a video game. After one year at Georgia Tech, he was picked fourth overall in the 1996 NBA Draft. In the NBA, he was selected as an All-Star in 2001 and 2003 and led his team to the playoffs five different times.

Marbury's résumé looked to be that of a great basketball star. But in reality, his story was one of controversy and rejection, at least in the NBA. As soon he entered the professional league, people started to notice his flashy me-first playing style and his frequent run-ins with coaches, and he quickly developed a reputation for being selfish. He was traded to four different teams before landing with the New York Knicks—a team he'd dreamed of playing for while growing up. Quickly, he came to blows with two different head coaches and was labeled "toxic," a "coach-killer," a "bonehead," and a "loser." He was regularly suspended and frequently booed by fans.

Despite putting up decent numbers, Marbury's reputation forced the New York Knicks to cut him. After spending a forgettable year with the Boston Celtics, he was essentially forced out of the league. Despite his immense talent, he was rejected by both the NBA and its fans after a tumultuous five-team, thirteen-year career. It looked as though his career was over for good.

Stephon Marbury could have simply lived off all the money he'd earned. Or he could have tried to latch onto another NBA team in an effort to extend his fading career. But he didn't do either of these things. Instead, he chose to step back and take his career to the other side of the globe—to China.

In the Chinese culture, which is much more reserved, Marbury's brassy manner and playing style were seen as much needed leadership for a basketball team. After two seasons in the Chinese Basketball Association (CBA), Marbury signed with the Beijing Ducks, a team that had never won a championship in the league's seventeen-year history, despite being one of the league's richest teams.

In Beijing, Marbury transformed from an NBA reject to a local legend. As the starting point guard, he averaged more than 30 points per game and led the Ducks to their first-ever championship in 2012. Before accepting the trophy, he was tossed in the air by his teammates. He then broke down in tears for more than fifteen minutes in the locker room. "This has been incredible," he kept repeating to the reporters.

Two years later, he led the Ducks to their second championship. At age thirty-seven, Marbury became a hero to Beijing's twenty million residents and received the "Beijing Honorary Citizen" award from its mayor. They even built a bronze statue in his likeness outside the stadium where the Ducks play. In every sense, Marbury went from fame to rejection, then back to fame again.

Say what you will about Marbury's personality, but his "switch up" illustrates that there is possibility after rejection—and that rejection is not always the end of the story. Hanging on for dear life and giving up by quitting are not the only two options left after a no. Instead, sometimes you need to step back and reevaluate your talents and dreams, as well as the conditions and the environment in which you have been trying to get an acceptance. By taking a look at all of the factors, you might be able to find a new approach that will allow you to see an idea in a new light—and get the yes you've always wanted.

## LESSONS

1. Ask "Why" Before Good-bye: Sustain the conversation after the initial rejection. The magic word is "why," which can often reveal the underlying reason for the rejection and present the rejectee with the opportunity to overcome the issue.

2. Retreat, Don't Run: By not giving up after the initial rejection, and instead retreating to a lesser request, one has a much higher chance of landing a yes.

3. Collaborate, Don't Contend: Never argue with the rejector. Instead, try to collaborate with the person to make the request happen.

4. Switch Up, Don't Give Up: Before deciding to quit or not to quit, step back and make the request to a different person, in a different environment, or under a different circumstance.

CHAPTER 7

# POSITIONING FOR YES

**T**HE STORY OF JIRO ONO, AN EIGHTY-FIVE-YEAR-OLD Japanese man who spent his entire life mastering and perfecting the art of making sushi, was brought to fame by the 2011 documentary *Jiro Dreams of Sushi*. His small restaurant in Tokyo had become the most famous sushi shop in the world and a national treasure for Japan, so much so that President Obama made a stop on his visit to the country and claimed it was the "best sushi I've ever had in my life."

One thing about Jiro's restaurant that amazed many viewers was the grueling and detailed basic skills training that Jiro's apprentices have to go through in order to work at the restaurant. They must first learn to properly hand-squeeze the hot towels the restaurant offers to patrons. The towels are so hot that they burn the apprentices' hands. After they

master that, they spend ten years learning to cut and prepare fish. After a decade of dealing with fish, they earn the
right to cook eggs. One apprentice explained that he had to
prepare more than two hundred batches of egg sushi over
several months before he was allowed to prepare it for customers.

Jiro's story shows the importance of learning the fun-
damentals before elevating to more complicated skills and
eventually mastering the whole art.

If my entire art was to handle rejection, then not giving
up after a no was like towel squeezing. I'd learned a lot, but
there was much more to come. The next step was to learn
different ways to position myself to receive more yeses in the
first place.

Since getting a yes involves persuasion, I vowed to not
tune down the craziness of my request to make it easy. I
didn't want to get a yes by making a cheap, obvious request;
I was already so much more confident than I had been at
the beginning of this journey that I didn't need to boost my
pride with easy yeses. Instead, I wanted to see if I could uncover some principles that would make a yes more likely, no
matter what kind of request it was attached to.

## GIVE MY "WHY"
### 100 DAYS OF REJECTION: GIVING $5 TO RANDOM PEOPLE IN AUSTIN, AND TAKING PICTURES WITH STRANGERS IN NEW YORK CITY

> *"The best things in life are free, but you can keep them for the birds and bees. Now give me money, that's what I want."*
>
> —BARRETT STRONG IN THE SONG "MONEY"

Is money what people really want over anything else, as suggested in Barrett Strong's classic song? If so, I figured that giving people money—with no strings attached—would be greeted with overwhelming acceptance. At least, that's what I was thinking when I positioned myself on a busy street corner in downtown Austin and offered $5 bills to random strangers walking by. I didn't tell them what I was doing. Instead, I just stood there with my hand out and asked them if they'd like five bucks, without giving them any reason.

In the interests of not draining my bank account, I offered the money to only five people. Here are the results:

Person #1: She was very happy and kept saying, "That was very sweet of you!" She also offered to "give it to somebody, too," when she saw a person in need.

Person #2: She eyed me with some suspicion and asked me if there was a catch to my offer. After hearing that there was no catch, she smiled and took the money—but told me to come back and pick it up if I needed it.

Person #3: He flatly refused the offer, saying, "I don't need $5." Before walking away, he pointed toward a nearby homeless shelter. "There are plenty of guys on the street who would die to have $5. Why don't you give it to them?"

Person #4: He asked me what the $5 was for. "Nothing," I said. He walked away quickly.

Person #5: She also asked me what it was for. Again, I said, "Nothing." She laughed uncomfortably and walked away.

In the end, two said yes, and three said no.


Soon after that, I took my visiting aunt on a trip to New York City—a city always bustling with people. Everywhere we went—Times Square, Central Park, the Empire State Building—we saw people posing for pictures. Many times, the person taking the photo would politely ask strangers to step out of the frame or simply wait until they'd passed by. It was as if everyone was striving to show they were the only people visiting these landmarks at that moment. Seeing this happen again and again, an idea came to mind. Since New Yorkers are as much a part of the fabric of New York as its buildings, why not ask random New Yorkers if I could pose with them on the street, with my aunt acting as the photographer?

Over the next few hours, I asked dozens of random people to pose with me. They varied widely by ethnicity, gender, and age. Some of them didn't speak English very well. The only common factor was how I approached them. I told them that I wanted to take a photo with them because I believed that people are an integral part of a city.

Some of them initially thought I asked them to take a picture *for* me and were surprised to find out I wanted them in the picture *with* me. Others showed a little hesitation at the beginning and paused to process my unusual request.

But the most surprised person of all was me, because every single one of them said yes.

Plenty of people think the reason I got so many yeses during my rejection journey is because I lived in Austin, Texas, a place with a reputation for outgoing, quirky residents. They figure it's a function of southern hospitality, and that if I made the same requests in place like New York or pretty much anywhere in Europe, I'd be sternly rejected.

In some cases, they might be right. But I had been rejected many times in Austin—sometimes when it was least expected, like when I'd tried handing out the $5 bills. But now here I was in New York, making a request that offered no benefit to anyone, and everyone I'd approached had agreed to pose for a picture.

At first glance, this made no sense. But after revisiting the videos, I saw one glaring difference between the New York photo request and the Austin money giveaway. In New York, I'd told each of those strangers on the sidewalk *why* I was asking them to pose with me in a photo—I wanted to include people, not just landmarks, in my photo. I hadn't left it to them to fill in the blanks when it came to my motivation. As a result, they responded positively, even though the request was outside the normal social behavior they were used to seeing every day.

I had begun to realize that asking people why after receiving a rejection helped me understand their reasoning and sometimes turn a no into a yes—or into an even more interesting offer. Now I was finding that explaining *my* why up front had a similar effect. I wasn't the first one to notice this.

In 1978, Harvard psychologist Ellen Langer conducted an experiment that revealed this very point. In the experiment, she approached people waiting to use a copy machine, asking them if she could cut in front of them to make copies herself. She wanted to see if the way that she worded the request had an effect on their response. When she said, "Excuse me, I have five pages. May I use the Xerox machine?," 60 percent of people allowed her to go ahead of them. When she added her reason, asking, "Excuse me, I have five pages. May I use the Xerox machine because I'm in a rush?," her yes rate increased to 94 percent. In her third variation, she also gave a reason, but purposely designed it to be ridiculous: "Excuse me, I have five pages. May I use the Xerox machine because I have to make some copies?" Shockingly, the number of people who accepted her request stayed about the same at 93 percent.

Langer's experiment—dubbed "The Copy Machine"—became a landmark study in psychology. It demonstrates that people's responses to a request are deeply influenced by knowing there is a reason behind it, no matter what that reason is. Everything I experienced during my rejection journey reinforced this. When I gave people a reason for my request, however far-fetched, I was far more likely to get a yes.

But lots of people miss this step—including me. Looking back, I'm amazed at how often I didn't offer a reason for my request, usually because I assumed the other person already knew it or wouldn't want to know it. Sometimes, I was so deeply embedded in what I was requesting that it didn't even occur to me that I needed to walk someone through my enthusiasm. Other times, revealing my rationale made me feel too vulnerable. And sometimes I wasn't sure about the reason or couldn't articulate it to myself.

## START WITH "I"

Of course, Langer's experiment only looked at the challenge from the perspective of the person asking the question. The reasons she gave originated from her desire and needs, however ludicrous or reasonable, and ignored the needs of the people who were already standing in the copy machine line. This got me wondering: What would happen if the why that I offered wasn't about me but more about *them*—the people to whom I was posing my requests?

In his classic bestselling book *How to Win Friends and Influence People*, Dale Carnegie advocates "becoming genuinely interested in other people" and "talking in terms of the other man's interest." What if I applied this to a rejection challenge? If the why that I gave was more about meeting the other person's interests and needs rather than my own, would that increase my chances of getting to yes?

## 100 DAYS OF REJECTION:
## GIVE A HAIRCUT TO A HAIRDRESSER

Not all my rejection attempts made it onto my video blog—and the Dale Carnegie–inspired rejection was one of them. That's because everything that could have gone wrong did go wrong, right from the start.

My idea was to stroll into a local hair salon and ask the hairdresser whether she might like me to cut her hair, as a way to break up the monotony of her day. So that's exactly what I did. After exchanging a few pleasantries with a hairdresser—a Vietnamese woman with very sharp scissors in her hands—I pitched her my request.

"May I cut your hair?" I asked.

"You want to cut my hair?" She gave me a slight smile, hinting at her amusement.

Then I followed up the question with what I somehow thought at the time was a great and generous why.

"Yes, I'm sure you have cut hair from thousands of heads and you must be bored with your job and wondering what it's like on the other side," I said. "I can cut your hair and make sure you look good."

The hairdresser, who clearly took pride in her job, turned her smile into a frown faster than I could finish my sentence.

"What do you mean I must be bored? I love my job!" she retorted.

The customer whose hair she was cutting sensed the hairdresser's unhappiness and gallantly jumped to her defense. He started swearing, accusing me of interrupting her work, and calling me unprintable names.

Admittedly, my request was bizarre. But I hadn't expected to be on the receiving end of a two-on-one confrontation. It was hard for me to keep calm amid all the name-calling and angry accusations. I tried to explain that all I wanted was to lighten the mood and make it fun, and I just wanted to cut even a strand of her hair.

But it was too late. No matter what I said, I couldn't change the chemistry of that conversation from contention to collaboration.

In the end, I apologized and left. I was in a rather foul mood, not because I got rejected but because a would-be fun experience had turned quickly into something rather unpleasant. I felt sorry for the hairdresser, whose happy day was interrupted by this exchange, all because I had said the wrong thing. Judging by her initial reaction, she might have even said yes if I had offered a genuine why.

Because of the customer's bad language, I never uploaded this video to my blog. The last thing I wanted was to use my social media presence to make someone look bad. I felt badly enough about the exchange as it was.

The "hairdresser incident" taught me some important lessons (not least of which, obviously, is to never underestimate the pride that a hairdresser takes in her job). But the real lesson was this: I didn't really know the hairdresser's interest and needs. Instead, I'd made some guesses in the moment that proved wildly incorrect. My manufactured reason had missed the mark by a mile. Why would a professional hairdresser let an untrained stranger cut her hair and risk messing it up? She also loved her job, and my suggestion that she could be "bored" and needed me to "lighten the mood" had been perceived as an insult. I am sure there are bored hairdressers out there who would enjoy a break from their routine, but she wasn't one of them, and I shouldn't have put a negative spin on her work either way.

Also, even if she had wanted a break, having a random guy cut her hair was probably the least-relaxing break she could imagine. Offering to perform a karaoke song for her or sweep her station might have gone over much better.

But what bothered me the most about the incident was the realization that I hadn't actually been thinking about the other person's needs. I'd wanted this rejection attempt to be about her but really, I hadn't proposed anything that might actually do her a favor. I was only asking to fulfill *my own desire* for a crazy request.

James Pennebaker, a social psychologist at the University of Texas at Austin, once conducted research on the way people use pronouns in their e-mails. He discovered that the more people use the pronoun "I," the more likely they are telling the truth and are perceived as such. On the other hand, the more people use "you" or "he/she/they" as the subject of a sentence, the more likely they are to be not telling the truth. No wonder that when banks or utility companies send out letters with unwelcome news, whether it's raising a fee or reducing a benefit, and they start out by saying "to better serve you," we never believe them.

When I'd asked to "borrow $100," "get a burger refill," or

"play soccer in your backyard," I hadn't attempted to come up with reasons to demonstrate how saying yes would benefit the other person. People, in turn, said either yes or no, but no one felt upset or talked down to. By starting my request with "I," I could ensure that others understood that I was asking them for a favor—not trying to do them a false favor that didn't ring true.

## ACKNOWLEDGE DOUBTS

The hairdresser incident once again brought up for me the issue of trust and comfort—one of the most important themes that ran through my whole rejection journey. I'd come to recognize a certain look that would pass over other people's faces as soon as they heard one of my requests. It was a combination of surprise, confusion, and suspicion. I could almost see them checking me out and asking themselves: *How do I know this guy has no unfriendly intentions? How do I know he isn't trying to sell me a bridge, recruit me to a cult, or steal my identity?* As a guy fighting my own rejection fear, I knew I meant no harm to the random people I approached. But how could I make sure that *they* knew it? How could I make them more comfortable when talking to me?

## 100 DAYS OF REJECTION: BE A STARBUCKS GREETER

I'm a big fan of "greeters"—those friendly, helpful people positioned inside the doors of giant big-box stores like Walmart, the ones who magically always know exactly where you can find what you're looking for. I've always appreciated being met by a "hi" when I walk into stores that might otherwise feel vast and daunting, and it certainly helps to have someone on hand to direct me.

But I don't shop at Walmart very often. Starbucks, on the other hand, is one of my favorite places to visit. I've always found them friendly and convenient—and I love the coffee. Starbucks doesn't have greeters, though, and I doubt it ever will. But it seemed like a good enough idea for me to turn it into a rejection attempt.

So I ventured into my local Starbucks one day and asked the barista if I could stand by the door for an hour or so as a "Starbucks greeter." The barista's name was Eric. Not surprisingly, he had a tough time making sense of my request. I could tell that he wanted to grant my wish, but he was also unsure of my intentions. Seeing his dilemma, I tried to make him more comfortable.

"Is that weird?" I asked him.

"Yeah, it's a little weird," he replied, almost with relief. But acknowledging what I was asking was strange seemed to put him at ease. "You aren't trying to sell anything, right?" he asked. He told me, then, that at some point they'd had a woman position herself at the door trying to sell products to incoming customers, and they'd had to ask her to leave. Eric didn't want a replay of that experience, and part of his hesitation was remembering that tricky situation.

I assured him that I wasn't trying to sell anything—I just really loved their coffee and wanted to help people enjoy the Starbucks experience even more. Ultimately, Eric conceded. "I don't see why not," he said. "As long as it doesn't get ridiculous."

For the next hour, I stood at the door and welcomed every customer who walked in with a greeting and a smile. I even tried out different phrases, like "Welcome to Starbucks!" and "We have the best coffee in the world!" Most people totally ignored me (though one customer did toast me with her coffee cup). But I didn't mind. As a greeter, I didn't need much to be happy.

Although it might seem counterintuitive, acknowledging other people's doubts can help rather than hurt your cause. Demonstrating to Eric that I knew that my request was "weird" actually gave me a different kind of credibility. For one, it proved to him that I wasn't crazy, and we were more or less on the same page. But it also revealed both honesty and empathy on my part, two feelings that are crucial to evoking trust. Asking "Is this weird?" put Eric more at ease and opened his mind to my request. It gave him an opportunity to be honest with me and explain what his reservations were. That conversation then gave me the opportunity to assure him that allowing me to be a greeter would not undermine him, his customers, or his store. In the end, it more than likely increased the possibilities of me getting a yes.

Though it sounds easy, preemptively acknowledging another person's doubts can be very hard to do in the heat of the moment. Before launching my rejection journey, whenever I'd ask other people for something—whether it was a job, venture funding, or to buy something that I was selling—I never wanted to bring up or discuss any underlying doubts and questions they might have. I thought doing so would undermine my cause and actually hand them a reason to say no to me. I hoped that by *not* mentioning their doubts, those doubts would simply go away, or at least remain hidden. But in most cases, other people's doubts do not disappear by themselves. Instead, they can linger and are more likely to become the very reason for a rejection if you don't take control of them.

Of course, I'm hardly the first person to discover that acknowledging others' doubts can strengthen rather than destroy your credibility. Companies play with this principle all the time. Take Domino's Pizza. In a 2009 survey of consumer taste preferences among national pizza chains, Domino's tied for last place with Chuck E. Cheese's. Soon after, Domino's completely retooled its pizza recipes and its menu. But the national advertising campaign that followed didn't tout the newness, freshness, and awesomeness of the new pizza. Instead, it brutally criticized the company's old products, sharing feedback from consumers that included words like *mass produced*, *boring*, *bland*, and *forgettable*.

I remember watching those ads and thinking that if Domino's was that honest about how bad its pizza used to be, then there must be something to its whole remake. I actually went to Domino's just to try out its new pizza for that reason. And I wasn't alone. The company's relaunch and honesty campaign proved a wild success. One year after the campaign and in the middle of the recession, Domino's revived its pizza business and experienced a historical 14.3 percent quarterly gain in sales—the highest jump ever by a major fast-food chain.

No matter the situation, bringing people's doubt out in the open can be a powerful way to gain their attention, their trust, and often even their acceptance. It also has a way of diffusing the fear and the nerves that you feel when making a request. By being "real" and acknowledging the skepticism that other people might feel, you can help put them at ease, *yourself* at ease, and boost your credibility at the same time.

Of course, it is possible that if I do everything right to put myself in the right position, including giving my reason, starting with "I," and acknowledging doubts, the other person could still reject me. Sometimes the other person will reject you no matter what, and sometimes he or she doesn't want or need what you are offering.

Yet there is one thing you can do to boost your chances of getting a yes. You can't change people—but you *can* select your target wisely.

## TARGET THE AUDIENCE
### 100 DAYS OF REJECTION: GIVING A COLLEGE LECTURE

My family tree is filled with teachers. In fact, my great-great-grandfather started one of the most influential Confucius academies in China 102 years ago. My grandparents, my father, and my uncles all taught in either colleges or high schools. I often joked that I might be the first true capitalist in my family, because I dreamed of becoming an entrepreneur instead of following my lineage and becoming another teacher. Though she never intended to put any pressure on me, as I grew up, my grandmother would once in a while mention that it would be great for me to become a teacher, too.

So I had always wondered what it was like to teach a college class. During my 100 Days of Rejection, I felt as if I had opened a window in my life to ask for anything I wanted. If I could get Olympic donuts or find a job in one afternoon, why not try to become a teacher for an hour?

I prepared a résumé and business card and created a lecture in PowerPoint on my iPad (my topic, of course, was how to handle rejection). Then, one afternoon, I put on my favorite dress shirt and headed to the University of Texas in Austin.

I started at the business school. I felt that with my background in being a former business school student and currently an entrepreneur, I could relate to these professors the best. However, I quickly found out that the school was on break and almost no professors were around. I grabbed a faculty directory and started to cold-call professors in other departments, just trying to talk to someone. I picked a school of communications professor named Dr. Joel Rollins. He taught a debate class at the time.

When he answered my call, he asked me if I was trying to sell anything. I assured him that I wasn't, but that I wanted to offer his students a lecture that might give them a new perspective on communication. Sounding suspicious but a little intrigued, Rollins told me he would give me five minutes of his time for an in-person meeting at his office.

During that meeting, I explained that I was a local entrepreneur and blogger. I pulled out my iPad and showed him the lecture on rejection I would give to his students if he said yes. He looked through it and seemed impressed by my preparation. He said the topic probably wasn't right for his debate class but might be useful for another class he would be teaching in the upcoming semester on communication and social change. Because "people in movements . . . get rejected a lot when they are trying to start something."

After a little more conversation, Rollins agreed to fit me into his curriculum. I couldn't believe I was about to make one of my dreams come true simply by asking. I was ready to give him a hug, but I restrained myself from showing too much enthusiasm. I learned my lesson about never going crazy in front of a professor during my college days.

A month later, when the new semester rolled around, Rollins called me to set up a time for my lecture. When I hung up the phone, I knew my moment had finally come.

My grandma once read me a touching short story when I was young. It was called "La Dernière Classe"—"The Last Lesson"—by Alphonse Daudet. The story was about a teacher and Frenchman named Monsieur Hamel giving his last class lecture to his students. France had lost the Franco-Prussian War and was forced to relinquish territory to its enemy. The next day the school would start teaching lessons in German instead of French. Monsieur Hamel dressed up for the occasion—and gave the best lecture of his life.

This wasn't my last lecture—it was my first. But I dressed up for the occasion as well, in my favorite shirt, like Monsieur Hamel did. In the class, I discussed how because people resist change, especially when it comes to power and tradition, the most important ideas and movements often encounter the most violent rejections. I cited examples of Apostle Paul and Dr. Martin Luther King Jr., and how they turned rejections into opportunities, and changed the world as a result. I encouraged the students not to give up easily in the face of nos, and to be smart to obtain yeses.

When the class was over, the students gave me a warm round of applause, and Professor Rollins engulfed me in a hug (now *that* was a surprise!). My wife, Tracy, was also there. As we walked out of the classroom together, I was wiping away tears. I felt my grandma's spirit was there in that classroom watching me that day. And I knew she was proud of me.

It was tough to analyze myself after such an emotional episode. To this day, I still can't believe that things that mean so much to me could happen that fast if I just asked for them. However, I know I did one thing that helped me, and it was one of the most important lessons I learned through my 100 Days of Rejection: target the right audience.

Before meeting Professor Rollins, I had spent days working on the lecture material I would be giving to hypothetical college students in a hypothetical class. I'd pictured myself as a professor, channeled my family tree, and put in my best work. I did all this without knowing if my presentation would ever be given or even seen by anyone. I also dressed the part and prepared a polished résumé that highlighted my experience—both of which brought me credibility during my encounter with Professor Rollins. I proved that I wasn't just a crazy guy with a crazy wish, or a jokester looking for a laugh.

Yet however well prepared I was, I knew the odds of convincing a professor to let a stranger lecture to his students were very low. To increase those odds, I aimed my request at what I hoped would be the most receptive audience. Thinking that the business school would probably value my message the most, I started there. When that didn't work out due to unfortunate timing, I moved to my next best choice—the communications school. Professor Rollins welcomed me with open arms, and so did his students. But had I picked a professor from the school of nursing, I might have gotten a swift rejection.

In other words, targeting is everything.

A few years ago, *Washington Post* columnist Gene Weingarten staged an intriguing experiment that quickly went viral. He asked Joshua Bell, a Grammy Award–winning violinist and conductor, to play his violin in a busy DC metro station dressed like a normal street fiddler. Bell is one of the most accomplished violinists in the world, and people pay hundreds of dollars to attend his concerts. Weingarten had him playing anonymously for a pack of busy commuters. Would they stop, recognize his genius, and count their lucky stars for being able to listen to a masterful performance for free? Or would they take no notice?

Wearing a T-shirt, jeans, and a baseball cap, Bell gave his best effort. During his forty-five-minute subway performance, 1,097 people passed by the spot where Bell was playing. Only seven stopped to listen, and only one recognized Bell.

Many attributed the results to the commuters' lack of interest in classical music or their narrow focus on their travel logistics. Another reason was Bell's anonymity—and thus his lack of credibility.

However, no one can deny the fact that the performance was targeted at the wrong audience. Just days before, Bell had performed at the prestigious John F. Kennedy Center to a standing ovation. The contrast couldn't be more stunning.

Of course, it's hard to draw a direct comparison between me trying to sell my first-ever attempt at teaching and a world-class violinist doing what he knows best. However, both these examples demonstrated the principle of targeting. It doesn't matter how amazing your performance or products are, if you target the wrong audience, who don't recognize, appreciate, or need your value, your effort will be both wasted and rejected.

## LESSONS

1. Give My "Why": By explaining the reason behind the request, one has a higher chance to be accepted.

2. Start with "I": Starting the request with the word "I" can give the requestor more authentic control of the request. Never pretend to think in the other person's interests without genuinely knowing them.

3. Acknowledge Doubts: By admitting obvious and possible objections in your request before the other person, one can increase the trust level between the two parties.

4. Target the Audience: By choosing a more receptive audience, one can enhance the chance of being accepted.

CHAPTER 8

# GIVING A NO

**A**FTER WEEKS FILLED WITH REJECTION ATTEMPTS, IT became a fun routine to get up every day looking for new ways to be rejected. There was still some fear here and there. But I was learning a tremendous amount about psychology, negotiation, and persuasion. And the challenge of constantly experimenting and testing out my growing knowledge—then sharing it with readers—still felt exhilarating. By Jiro Ono's measure, I was ready to start serving egg sushi to customers.

Still, I found myself wondering if I was nearing some sort of peak—if the rate of my learning might slow down because I'd squeezed all the learning there was out of rejection.

That might have been true, if not for a minicrisis that was brewing in my life.

I was still getting lots of e-mails and comments from readers and viewers through social media, and sorting through all of them had become a full-time job all its own. I truly felt honored that so many people wanted to share their life stories with me, or ask me questions about my experiences. I appreciated them reaching out and really enjoyed the interaction and learning that came from helping others.

But because I'd gone so public with my fight with rejection—and had become a pretty vocal advocate of not being afraid to ask for things—I also found myself on the receiving end of a lot of requests. People started asking me for personal coaching sessions, for jobs, and to enter into business partnerships with them. Some of the requests were pretty outlandish. One person asked me to market his produce, and another wanted to hang out with me at his house for a weekend. Many of these requests started with, "Jia, since you taught me not to be afraid of rejection, here is my own version of rejection therapy. Would you [insert request]?"

At first, I said yes to everything that seemed doable. But as time went on, fulfilling these requests started to dominate my life. I had less and less time for my blog, my family, and myself. The sheer volume of requests started to weigh on me, and it made me less enthusiastic in my responses. With so many people wanting something from me, sometimes I said yes but didn't do a great job of following through, and that bothered me, too.

Eventually, I realized that I had to start saying no to people just to restore balance to my life. And that wasn't fun at all.

Given my lifelong fear of rejection, it is probably no surprise that I have never liked saying no to people. Being the person *doing* the rejection didn't feel much better to me than being on its receiving end. In fact, it made me feel like a jerk. Once I got deep into my rejection journey, saying no also made me feel like a hypocrite. Here I was, teaching people to ask for what they want and then not saying yes to them. I hated it.

Moreover, I was really, really bad at saying no. People would send me letters or requests that were paragraphs long. Replying with a short and quick "sorry, I can't do it" felt disrespectful by comparison. But matching the time and effort they put into crafting these requests was impossible. I simply didn't know what to do.

Bad habits set in. I started delaying my responses, telling myself that I'd get to them later. Sometimes I would forget about them altogether. But in my mind, I always had that nagging feeling that I owed some people something, and many times I had a hard time sleeping because of it. Soon, whenever I received an e-mail from someone that contained a request, I felt dread rather than excitement.

One day I happened to be visiting a college friend. It had been a decade since we had last seen each other, and we were both very happy to be meeting up. Back then, she'd shared with me her dream of becoming a mom and running her own nonprofit organization for women in need. She had finished both college and graduate school with that latter aim in mind. Sure enough, she was now the mom of two beautiful daughters. While she didn't run her own nonprofit, she volunteered with several organizations doing social good. But she was far from living her dream.

My friend confided with me how much she had to do

as a volunteer. The organizations she worked with all had great intentions and noble goals, but the people in charge would often rather have someone else do the hard work— specifically, her. When they asked her to put in more hours than her fair share, she didn't know how to say no. But when she took on everything, her resentment would start to build. Whenever she did manage to say no, it confused her coworkers because it was not consistent with what she had done in the past. This dilemma had soured her on the work she was doing—and even on her dream. She told me she was ready to quit and take a break from it all.

My friend's revelation shocked me, not only because it was sad to see her unhappy but also because of how similarly we felt about not being able to say no to others' well-intentioned requests. I realized that if I didn't get a handle on my reluctance to reject people, then I might end up wanting to quit as well. I might even accidentally sabotage the work that I was doing—because at the root of the problem was the same issue I'd been battling all along: my fear of rejection. I wasn't afraid to say no. I was afraid of people's reactions—specifically, their disappointment and anger. Put another way, I was afraid they would reject me because of my rejection.

So I started looking back through my videos, examining how all the people I'd approached had delivered their rejections. I quickly found out that not all rejections were created equal. There were good rejections and bad rejections. Some of the people who had rejected me had been harsh and dismissive, but others had said no with such finesse and kindness that they managed to make me like them despite their nos. These "good" rejectors had something to teach, and I watched those videos again and again until I had fully absorbed their lessons.

## 100 DAYS OF REJECTION: EXCHANGE SERVICES WITH A PERSONAL TRAINER

One of the videos I studied the most was the rejection attempt I made with a personal fitness trainer named Jordan.

In ancient times, before the introduction of currency, bartering was one of the main systems people used to exchange goods and services. In today's world dominated by credit cards and digital transactions, I wondered if bartering would still work even in isolated instances. So I turned it into a rejection attempt.

My goal was to get a personal trainer to give me an hour of free training without me joining his gym. In exchange, I would offer to spend an hour teaching him everything I'd learned about entrepreneurship and blogging.

I walked into a local 24 Hour Fitness and started looking around for my target. That's when I spotted Jordan, a tall, young guy with bulging biceps.

Jordan listened patiently to my request to exchange services, then quickly explained that he couldn't accept the trade because of company policy, which prevented him from giving out free trainings. But Jordan was a helpful guy. He suggested that if I joined 24 Hour Fitness as a member, I could get a free hour of training as part of the gym's "fitness orientation."

I didn't want to join the gym—that would sort of defeat

the purpose. So I made a strategic retreat and tried a different approach. "If you can't do it here, can we go somewhere else to do this?"

Jordan shook his head, looking truly sorry. He'd signed a noncompete clause, he told me, and would get fired for doing training anywhere outside the gym on his own.

I definitely didn't want to get Jordan fired. But before leaving, I did want to know whether my original offer was valuable to him at all. "Are you interested in entrepreneurship and blogging?" I asked.

"No. I'm really not. I'm pursuing a firefighting career," Jordan replied.

"That's a great career," I told him, and I meant it. "I have huge respect for firefighters. They are heroes!"

"Thanks, I appreciate that," Jordan replied. Then he did something totally unexpected.

"I have a card of a friend who has her own gym," he told me. "I know they have trainers in there so you can always stop by. They are not under contract with any other gym, and they are a private entity. Maybe they can do it."

He found his friend's business card and handed it to me. I called the number on the card and soon found myself with an offer to work out for free at his friend's gym.

Jordan's generosity wasn't what stuck with me. What amazed me was the way he'd rejected my initial request. He wasn't dismissive, even though my request held no interest for him. He heard me out, and showed that he was taking me seriously by giving me real reasons why the request wasn't going to work. He made me feel valued by pulling out his problem-solving skills and doing what he could to help me get what I wanted. Jordan's no felt very much like a yes. Indeed, Jordan had delivered a "perfect rejection."

## PATIENCE AND RESPECT

What impressed me the most about Jordan was his attitude toward me as a person. No matter how many times or how many ways I tried to get what I wanted, his demeanor remained calm and respectful—and it's hard to be unhappy when the other person is being nice the whole time. Being patient and respectful when saying no is such a simple concept. But it's amazing how often we *don't* put it into practice.

Consider the story of Kelly Blazek, a marketing and communications executive. A few years ago, Blazek created the Cleveland Job Bank, a Yahoo! group that helps connect Cleveland-based marketing and communications job seekers with jobs in their field. The group has more than seventy-three hundred subscribers, many of whom have Blazek to thank for helping them find a job. Her work was even recognized by the International Association of Business Communicators (IABC), one of the most prestigious organizations in her field. In 2013, IABC named Blazek "Communicator of the Year."

Given all this, it's hard not to picture Blazek as a warm and helpful person and a great communicator. But in early 2014, Blazek shot to Internet notoriety when a nasty e-mail she sent went viral.

In response to a stranger's request to connect on LinkedIn, Blazek went ballistic.

"Your invite to connect is inappropriate, beneficial only

to you, and tacky," she wrote. "Wow, I cannot wait to let every 26-year-old jobseeker mine my top-tier marketing connections to help them land a job." And that was just the warm-up. "I love the sense of entitlement in your generation," she continued. "You're welcome for your humility lesson for the year. Don't ever reach out to senior practitioners again and assume their carefully curated list of connections is available to you, just because you want to build your network. . . . Don't ever write me again."

The recipient of Blazek's blazing rejection e-mail was Diana Mekota, a job seeker who planned to move to Cleveland and had been looking into joining Blazek's Yahoo! group. Obviously, Mekota was not happy about the letter. She published it on Twitter and Reddit, where thousands of people viewed it. They blasted Blazek for her arrogance and rudeness, and many even categorized her letter as cyberbullying. Other letters that she had written started to emerge, like this one, to someone who had failed to indicate what industry the person was in: "Am I a mind reader? . . . I promise to deny any requester who made me guess what they do. Congratulations—you're another one."

And this one, sent in response to an applicant who complained about her tone: "Since my tone is so off-putting, I think you'll be happier with the other Job Bank in town. Hint: there isn't one. You have a great day."

Facing a landslide of scrutiny, Blazek had to publicly apologize to Mekota and delete all her social media accounts. She even returned her 2013 "Communicator of the Year" award to IABC.

It was hard not to compare what had happened to Blazek

to what had happened to Jackie and me with our "Olympic donuts" moment. Magnified by the power of social media, the rude rejection cost Blazek her reputation and trashed the goodwill she'd spent years building as a volunteer. By contrast, Jackie's kindness in response to my request had the opposite effect, letting the whole world see just how amazing she was.

Of course, the difference between a good interaction and a bad one isn't always so dramatic. Sometimes the two are separated by nothing but a smile. At one point during my rejection journey, I visited a bookstore and asked two clerks if I could borrow a book instead of buying one. They both said no and explained the obvious reason. But one of them said it with a grumpy and annoyed look, adding, "I don't know what else to tell you." The other person said it with a smile. Next time I need to ask a question at a store, I'm certainly going to look for somebody with a smile on their face!

Showing patience and respect can soften the blow of rejection, and sometimes even earn the other person's respect and understanding. But a snarky attitude yields the opposite. It inflicts unnecessary harm on the other person—and, occasionally, exposes you to their irrational revenge, as in the case of Kelly Blazek.

Moral of the story: If you have to reject someone, do it nicely.

## BE DIRECT

In addition to his politeness, another thing that impressed me about Jordan was his directness. When I asked him if he was interested in blogging, he stated clearly that he wasn't. He didn't show fake interest. As a result, I respected his rejection—and him as a person as well.

I haven't always been a practitioner of this approach. Many times when I have had to say no to someone, I have delayed and procrastinated. Then I'd try to find the least painful way to deliver my rejection. This approach is usually counterproductive. A lot of people have the tendency to give indirect, sugarcoated rejections. They usually come in two forms: big setups and yes-buts.

With "big setups," rejectors spend a long time explaining the reason for their rejection before they actually deliver it. Companies are notoriously good at this.

In July 2014, Microsoft laid off 12,500 employees from its Nokia mobile phone division. To deliver the bad news to his employees, the head of the division, Stephen Elop, sent employees an eleven-hundred-word memo.

Elop began the memo casually with "Hello there." Then he spent ten paragraphs explaining Microsoft's new strategy, plan, and focus, the iconic nature of its products, the shifts in market, and the needs to selectively "right-size" the company.

Finally, in paragraph 11, Elop delivered the bad news:

"We plan that this would result in an estimated reduction of 12,500 factory direct and professional employees over the next year. These decisions are difficult for the team, and we plan to support departing team members with severance benefits."

I believe Elop had the right intention—to soften the blow of the layoff, which is among the worst professional rejections. But as successful as Elop had been as a corporate executive, he was afraid to give a straightforward rejection. So he painstakingly used reason and logic to set up the news, perhaps hoping the employees would be so convinced by the time they read the bad news that the blow would be lessened.

If Elop's goal was to use the memo to set up a smooth mass layoff, it didn't work. The laid-off employees didn't gush over Elop's essay. Instead, hundreds of them set up some very ugly protests.

Layoffs happen all the time. But Elop's approach caused a PR nightmare. The media took the memo public, writing stories with headlines like "Microsoft Lays Off Thousands with Bad Memo" and "How Not to Cut 12,500 Jobs: A Lesson from Microsoft's Stephen Elop."

The second form of indirect rejection is even more frustrating. "Yes-buts" happen when the rejector verbally acknowledges or even validates a request, then uses the word *but* or *unfortunately* to deliver the rejection.

Who hasn't called a customer support number, only to hear something like: "Yes, I understand that you are frustrated with these extra fees, and you want them to be taken off. And we value your business and try to provide the best

service possible. *Unfortunately,* we are unable to accommodate your request at this time."

"Yes-but" rejectors seem as if they are being polite and
acknowledging the other person's concerns and frustrations.
Yet the word *but*—and especially the word *unfortunately*—
totally undermine the rejector's good intentions. Apple con-
siders the word *unfortunately* so detrimental in customer
service that employees (or "geniuses") at the famously
customer-focused Apple Stores are banned from using it
when talking to customers.

In his book *Conversation Transformation*, organizational
consultant Ben E. Benjamin (that's his actual name) dis-
cusses the danger of "yes-buts." Not only do they send mixed
messages, he says, but also they make the idea difficult for
the rejectee's brain to process and could elicit a defensive response.

Last, when a rejector starts a sentence with "Yes, it is
true that . . . ," "Yes, I understand that . . . ," or "Yes, I know
that . . . ," the rejectee already senses that a "but" or an "unfortunately" is coming. He or she then ignores everything
the rejector is saying, painfully anticipating the upcoming
rejection and even forming a response.

When you deliver a rejection to someone, give the bad
news quickly and directly. You can add the reasons afterward, if the other person wants to listen. No one enjoys rejection, but people particularly hate big setups and "yes-buts."
They don't lessen the blow—in fact, they often do quite the
opposite.

## OFFER ALTERNATIVES

### 100 DAYS OF REJECTION:

### SPEAKING OVER COSTCO'S INTERCOM

I was shopping at a store with my family one day when a voice came on over the intercom. "Attention, shoppers, the store will be closing in five minutes; please bring your cart to the front." Knee-deep in my rejection journey at the time, I was looking for every opportunity to make a rejection request. I immediately knew what I wanted to try next.

The next time I went to a store, I told a random employee that I'd like to use the store's intercom system to make an announcement. She immediately referred me to the store manager, a middle-aged man named Robert. When I told him what I wanted—basically, for him to let me praise the store for its fabulous service over the loudspeaker—he looked at me closely, as if assessing whether or not I was serious.

"Unfortunately, I can't," he said. "We aren't allowed to."

I showed him my membership card. "I have spent thousands of dollars here," I told him. "There is no downside for you, really. If you say yes, everyone here will be happy." As speeches go, this was a little dramatic, but it was a throw-in-the-kitchen-sink moment. I could feel Robert slipping away.

He looked at me and shook his head. "Listen, I would love to do it, believe me. But unfortunately I can't."

But then, rather than walking away, Robert surprised me. "Are you hungry?" he asked.

It was my turn to be confused. I stood there, not knowing what to say.

"Come on, I will buy dinner for you and your family," he said.

Then he walked over with me to the food court. "Give him whatever he wants," he told the clerk, adding that it was for "member satisfaction."

After I ordered a pizza and a hot dog, Robert explained that he had really wanted to say yes, because he thought word-of-mouth marketing was the best kind of advertising. He said that while the company wouldn't allow a customer to speak over the intercom, it did have a membership magazine that would probably love to hear my story.

I opted to tell the story on my blog rather than share it in the magazine. But I appreciated Robert's attempt to come up with an alternative to my desired intercom moment. A few weeks later, after posting the Costco video to my blog, I went back to the store. Robert spotted me and came over to shake my hand. Quite a few shoppers had seen the hidden video, he said, and had stopped him in the store to say hi. I was happy that my blog post gave him the opportunity to be appreciated by customers. He deserved it.

The Costco rejection attempt not only gave me a full stomach, but also taught me a great way to reject someone: by offering an alternative. Robert could have just said no. Instead, he was patient and respectful and gave me real reasons for his no. Notice here that he did give me a yes—but with the word *unfortunately*. But then he offered a free dinner that I hadn't even asked for. How could I not be a fan of Robert and Costco after that?

Jordan at 24 Hour Fitness also offered me an alternative by directing me to his friend's gym. So had the gray-haired man who didn't want a rosebush in his yard, by sending me to someone who ultimately loved the offer.

These examples have something else in common—something very important. In each case, the person rejecting me was making it clear that he was rejecting my request—not rejecting me as a person. It can be hard, once you're rejected, to separate the two. In fact, one of the reasons people hate rejection so much is because they can't actually draw this distinction in their minds. They can't separate the rejection from who they are as a person. It takes practice and conscious thinking to separate the two and not take things personally.

However, by offering alternatives when rejecting someone, the rejector does this job on behalf of the rejectee. He or she is really saying, "Sorry, I can't do what you want, but it's really not because I don't trust or like you."

Rejection is a deeply personal experience, no matter who you are or what you have invested in the answer. So when you are rejecting something, you have to be specific. Make sure the person knows what exactly you're turning down, and be honest about the reasons why. This will save everyone a lot of time, trouble, and heartbreak.

## LESSONS

1. Patience and Respect: Rejection is usually a hard message. Delivering the message with the right attitude can go a long way to soften the blow. Never belittle the rejectee.

2. Be Direct: When giving a rejection, present the reason after the rejection. Avoid long and convoluted setup and reasoning.

3. Offer Alternatives: By offering alternatives to get a yes, or even simple concessions, one can make the other person a fan even in rejection.

CHAPTER 9

# FINDING UPSIDE

ONE OF MY FAVORITE POETS IS LU YOU. BORN IN CHINA in AD 1125, Lu was a child prodigy with an uncanny writing talent who started crafting poems at age twelve. When he was twenty-nine, he took first place in the Imperial Exam, a national standardized test given once every three years. In ancient China, the Imperial Exam was a big deal. The highest scorer usually became the emperor's favorite new cabinet member. Winning the exam could transform the fate of a person and his family for generations to come.

When Lu took first place, it seemed like he was headed for a life of power, wealth, and glory. But there was one problem. On the exam, Lu placed one spot higher than the grandson of Qin Hui—the most corrupt and powerful government official in the country and perhaps the most infamous in Chinese history. Qin was enraged that someone could dare to score higher than his beloved grandson. So he used his influence to remove Lu's name from the final ranking.

While Qin managed to block Lu's victory, he could not stop his writing. Over the years, Lu continued to write poems that expressed his ambitions and aspirations for the country. His writings became so influential and celebrated that they eventually caught the attention of the emperor, who granted Lu the cabinet position he had always desired.

But Lu's story didn't end there. Soon, the problem of being "too good" once again changed Lu's fate. His intolerance for corruption and his tough foreign policy stance didn't sit well with many established government officials. They ostracized him and spread rumors to impugn his character. Eventually the emperor turned on Lu as well, removing him from his cabinet.

Again jobless and disappointed, Lu went back to the countryside and picked up his pen. His writings about patriotism and rejection during this period became some of the most influential in Chinese literary history. His beautiful ways of capturing the pain of rejection—and the discovery of hope— are part of what drew me to his work.

One line in particular kept coming back to me throughout my 100 Days of Rejection: "After endless mountains and rivers that leave doubt whether there is a path out, suddenly one encounters the shade of a willow, bright flowers, and lovely village."* It was a parable about the ups, the downs, and the breathtaking discoveries Lu encountered in his own life.

* Translation by U.S. Secretary of State Hillary Clinton at the U.S. Pavilion at the Shanghai Expo, May 22, 2010.

Friedrich Nietzsche famously wrote: "That which does not kill us makes us stronger." This is very true when it comes to rejection. Everyone gets rejected countless times over the course of their lifetime. Ultimately, few if any of these rejections will prove life-threatening or fate-altering. Yet nearly every one of them offers us an opportunity to grow, to challenge ourselves, and to overcome the fears and insecurities that block us from meeting our full potential. Indeed, one of the greatest lessons of my journey was that any rejection can have hidden upsides, if only we are willing to look for them.

## MOTIVATION

One of the biggest upsides of rejection is that it can serve as motivation. And for me, the motivation came early.

My first big rejection came in elementary school.

My teacher, Ms. Qi, was full of love and genuinely cared about all her students. One day, she planned a big party for us. She bought all forty of us gifts, which she carefully wrapped and displayed at the front of classroom. During the party, Ms. Qi had all of us stand together in front of the room. One by one, each of us was supposed to offer another student a compliment. The student who received the compliment could then pick out a gift and go back to his or her seat. It was a thoughtful idea. What could possibly go wrong?

Standing in the group, I gave my heartiest cheers each time someone received a compliment and picked up his or her gift. Eventually, the group started to thin, and I was still standing there. My cheers became less and less enthusiastic, and gradually my joy turned into worry. Why hadn't anyone raised their hand and said something nice about me?

Then the group became really thin, and my worry sharpened into fear. There were just three students left—two unpopular kids nobody liked, and me. Everyone else was back in their seats, holding gifts wrapped in shiny paper. The three of us just stood there, and none of the other kids raised their hands.

Again and again, Ms. Qi asked—even implored—the class to offer us some praise, or just say anything, so she could get us off the platform that felt like a guillotine. Tears ran down my face, and I felt I'd rather die than remain standing there. Before that moment, I hadn't known I was that unpopular. But looking at who was standing beside me, I knew then.

Mercifully, Ms. Qi ended the horror show and asked us to pick up a gift and sit back down. I was too little to imagine what must have been going through her caring and gentle mind, having unknowingly turned a morale-building exercise into a public roasting of three kids without the appropriate comedy. Today, I feel worse for her than I did at that moment for myself, because she must have felt terrible for what she had accidentally set in motion.

This type of humiliation could leave a dark mark on a person in some way, especially a young kid like me. It could have changed who I was in ways that weren't good. I could have started trying harder to be accepted by everyone, and shaped my personality and interests to everyone's liking, in the hopes that conformity could prevent this type of traumatic rejection from happening again. Or I could have turned the tables and started hating everyone and the world. I could have become a bitter loner of the type causing a lot of tragic headlines nowadays.

Luckily, I chose a third route. Rather than feel humiliated by how different I was from the other kids, I embraced it. Standing in front of my classmates, none of whom would stick up for me, didn't make me feel vengeful. It made me want to prove everyone wrong about me—and show them who I really was.

In a strange way the experience also made me feel . . . special. From a very early age, I felt like I wasn't like everybody else. I didn't even *want* to be like everybody else. I wanted to find my own path. It's why I've always been drawn to figures like Thomas Edison and Bill Gates and other trailblazers who don't fit into neat molds. It's also why, over the years, whenever I've gone down a road that was different from the more conventional paths of my sixth-grade classmates—whether it was moving to America, going to college, or even having success with my blog—I always look back at that rejection with gratitude.

I learned something critical that day, though I didn't know it at the time and wouldn't really discover it until I started my rejection journey. What I learned is this: rejection is an experience that it is up to you to define. In other words, it means only what you choose it to mean. The relationship you have with a rejection can be negative or positive, and it all depends on which way you spin it for yourself.

Some people are extremely good at turning rejection into a positive, even if the·rejection itself still feels awful. They use the experience of rejection to strengthen and motivate themselves. Just ask Michael Jordan.

The speeches given at award ceremonies are usually heartfelt outpourings filled with thank-yous to families and supporters. They are usually emotional—and often a little boring. But Michael Jordan's 2009 Basketball Hall of Fame induction speech was anything but boring. In fact, it was unlike anything I've ever heard.

Over the span of twenty-three minutes, Jordan methodically listed every personal rejection he'd ever experienced in his career and explained how much it had fueled him—from his high school coach not picking him for the varsity team to his college roommate being named Carolina Player of the Year instead of him; from the opponent's coach who prohibited his team from fraternizing with Jordan to the media naysayers who claimed he wasn't as talented as Magic Johnson or Larry Bird. Jordan's speech revealed a side of him that his carefully crafted PR image had successfully hidden from the world—how he consistently used rejection as motivation during his career and even into retirement.

Jordan said that each rejection had "put so much wood on that fire that it kept me, each and every day, trying to get better as a basketball player. . . . For someone like me, who achieved a lot over the course of my career, you look for any kind of messages that people may say or do to get you motivated to play the game of basketball at the highest level, because that is when I feel like I excel at my best."

Jordan is not alone. The more I looked into it, the more I

was astonished by how many—and how often—successful people convert rejection into personal fuel.

• Quarterback Tom Brady was passed over 198 times in the 2000 NFL draft before finally being selected by the New England Patriots. He had already left the draft party dejected and crying. Brady has since become one of the greatest quarterbacks of all time, winning three Super Bowls and counting. He frequently cites his draft experience as part of what motivated him to succeed in the NFL and prove his worth to the teams that rejected him.

• An adopted child, Apple founder Steve Jobs was told by a playmate that he was unwanted and abandoned. According to his biographer Walter Isaacson, Jobs was deeply shaken by the comment, saying that "lightning bolts went off in my head. I remember running into the house. I think I was crying." After his parents assured him that they specifically selected him as their son, he realized that "I was not just abandoned. I was chosen. I was special." This shift in perspective became a core belief that helped drive him to unprecedented creative heights.

• After narrowly losing the presidency to George W. Bush in the 2000 election, former vice president Al Gore shifted his focus to the issue of climate change. His highly influential documentary on the issue, *An Inconvenient Truth*, won an Academy Award and altered the discourse on climate issues. Gore has referred to his election loss as a "hard blow" that "brought into clear focus the mission [he] had been pursuing for all these years."

• While at Disney, executive Jeffrey Katzenberg was rejected by his longtime boss, Michael Eisner, as Eisner's number two in command. In an interview with the *New York Times*, Katzenberg explained: "I ran the full gamut of emotions. I was disappointed, sad, angry, scared, philosophical, sad, vengeful, relieved, and sad." But Katzenberg used the rejection as motivation to start his own film company, DreamWorks, whose animated films grossed even more than films by Disney's Pixar by 2010. There was speculation that Katzenberg even modeled Lord Farquaad, the chief villain in DreamWorks's blockbuster animation movie *Shrek*, after Eisner.

Of course, the sting of rejection is not the only thing driving the work and the ambition of these and other highly successful people. Sooner or later, other intrinsic motivations such as "the love of the game" or the desire to "put a dent in the universe" need to take over to sustain excellence. But it's interesting to think about what might have happened if any of them had allowed rejection to deflate their sense of self—viewing it as something blocking their path rather than something they were eager and determined to overcome. Each of them saw rejection as "wood on the fire," as Michael Jordan so eloquently put it. It simply added more flame to the ambition they already had brewing.

## SELF-IMPROVEMENT

### 100 DAYS OF REJECTION: SOLICITING MONEY ON THE STREET

My hardest rejection attempts were the ones that were very public, where I opened myself to the possibility of being rejected not by one person but by dozens, or hundreds, or worse. This was why making an announcement on my Southwest flight to Vegas practically caused me to break out in hives. It's also why my elementary school rejection left such an impression.

The good thing about thinking up my own rejection attempts was that I knew exactly how to push my own rejection panic buttons. And I could think of no better way to terrify myself than to stand at a busy Austin intersection, holding up a sign asking strangers for money.

I drive by panhandlers almost every day, and I have never been able to even imagine what it would be like to be in their shoes. Does their need for money override their fear of being judged and rejected? Do time and experience erode the fear and shame? Or do they have a different relationship with rejection altogether?

I didn't want to be dishonest and stand on a corner claiming that I needed money. So I decided instead to ask for donations to a local food bank.

We often hear that real estate is about location, location, and location, and I figured that panhandling must follow the same rule. So I used Google Maps for my location research and picked a busy intersection just off one of Austin's main highways. Standing there, I saw the world the way a panhandler would view it every day, with cars driving by and stopping at the red light, their drivers seeing me through their windshields, making quick judgments, and usually lowering their heads to avoid eye contact. It was silent rejection by the masses and felt strangely reminiscent of my elementary school roast.

I felt trapped between wanting to draw people's attention and hoping to avoid their judgment. It felt impossibly painful. I resorted to all types of coping techniques to get through it—talking to myself, trying to hold a big smile, and imagining what the donations I got could do for hungry people, who otherwise might have to do this themselves.

Initially, I held up a sign that read: EVERYTHING GOES TO CHARITY! THANKS. I thought the sign was simple and to the point. But fifteen minutes passed, forty-eight cars came and went, and no one lowered his or her window or showed any interest in what I was doing. As the old adage goes, "When advertising fails, don't blame the customers. Blame the message."

I decided the message on my sign was too vague. So I changed it to something more specific, and hopefully more credible.

The new sign read: EVERYTHING GOES TO THE AUSTIN FOOD BANK! THANKS. Immediately, I got some results. A woman named Lisa rolled down her window, flashed a big smile, and said "bless you" while handing me $2. Another driver named Lori gave me $7, the highest amount I would collect from anybody. I held that sign for fifteen minutes. All in all, forty-three drivers saw me with the sign, but just two—Lisa and Lori—offered a donation.

Then I changed the sign again, this time emphasizing even more that the money I was collecting would go to a good cause—and not into my pocket. The third sign read: THIS IS NOT FOR ME! EVERYTHING GOES TO THE AUSTIN FOOD BANK! THANKS.

Two drivers, Jessica and John, offered me a handful of coins. Another woman handed me some money without stopping, making it hard to catch. A driver named Lindsey advised me to hold my sign horizontally, instead of vertically, so people could see me better. She didn't donate any money, but she didn't charge me a consulting fee either, so that was good. Another driver asked me for directions to the food bank, because he needed the help himself. It felt good to help someone in need.

In the end, sixty-six drivers saw the third sign during the fifteen minutes I held it, and three people donated a total of $6.73.

Then I changed the sign one more time, this time hoping to add a bit of humor. The new sign read: GOOGLE SUGGESTED HERE. EVERYTHING GOES TO THE AUSTIN FOOD BANK! THANKS!

The idea was to convey that Google Maps suggested this location for my panhandling excursion. Unfortunately, this last sign was like a bad insider joke, and it only confused people. In my final fifteen minutes, thirty-eight cars saw me, and no one gave me a dime. My poor messaging and bad attempt at humor proved counterproductive.

But in the end, I had a productive hour. I encountered a total of 195 cars and received five donations for a total of $15.73, which I happily gave to the Austin Food Bank online.

I learned a lot from this rejection attempt about the importance of good messaging (including the upside of being specific), the element of surprise, and the hard lesson of not confusing people with bad humor. But the biggest lesson of all was how to use rejection as a tool to learn, adapt, and improve. Instead of sulking, just hanging on, or simply giving up after the first fifteen minutes, I treated the experience as a feedback tool, and quickly changed my tactics without abandoning the cause altogether.

Using customer feedback to quickly build and improve products is standard practice for many businesses. They set up metrics to measure how customers use their product or behave under certain conditions, and the feedback they get can change the direction of a product or even an overall business.

Yet that same nimble mind-set is rarely brought to bear when it comes to rejection. Blinded by their own expectations and emotions, rejectees often fail to take advantage of the feedback given by a rejector. In Chapter 6, I talked about the importance of asking and understanding the why of rejection. If that's not possible, you can still change a component of a request and use people's rejections as a way to adjust your approach. The key is to withdraw yourself from the emotion as much as you can and approach your request more like a bold, creative experiment.

For example, in a job search, if you applied one hundred times with the same résumé and were rejected for an interview each time, instead of seeing the rejections as a sign that you are not qualified for the job and should lower your expectations, you could improve your résumé, write a new cover letter, or use other channels such as networking to try again and see if there is any change in the percentage of callbacks.

## WORTHINESS

When we think of rejection, we automatically assume it's a setback, a source of pain, and something we have to overcome. We rarely investigate the possibility that rejection, in some cases, is a result of being ahead of a curve.

Throughout history, we've seen countless examples of people who were rejected or even persecuted for their beliefs but vindicated by time. We've seen stories ranging from Galileo's scientific theories being declared heretical to Vincent van Gogh, whose work now sells for millions but who was deemed a failure during his own lifetime, to the biblical story of Noah, who was mocked for building an ark to prepare for a historic flood. Even in today's world, good ideas can face an uphill climb in many instances, especially if these ideas are creative in nature.

Companies, organizations, parents, teachers, and our society as a whole universally praise creativity and thinking outside of the box. However, when creativity actually happens, it is often met with rejection, because it frequently disrupts order and rules.

In the classic business book *The Innovator's Dilemma*, Harvard professor Clayton Christensen argued that companies often fail to innovate because they focus on currently profitable projects and reject internal innovations. As a result, they fall victim to disruptive innovation by outsiders, who are often small start-ups and don't have to worry about the status quo.

A study done by University of Pennsylvania psychologist Jennifer Mueller is called *The Bias Against Creativity: Why People Desire but Reject Creative Ideas*. Mueller found that no matter how much we say we love creativity on a conscious level, we subconsciously despise and fear it because it presents a level of uncertainty. As human beings, we crave certain and predictable outcomes. And we have tendencies to cling onto traditions and conventional wisdom. That's why there hasn't been any world-changing idea in history that was initially met with universal approval.

Looking back at my own journey, very few people gave me a chance to succeed when I quit my job to pursue an entrepreneurial dream. When I was rejected with the funding of my company, I did something unheard of. I spent part of the precious little time left in my six-month period to start a new video blog focused on my rejection. I did it because I felt the need to, and I didn't consult with anyone else. Later on, one of my best friends told me that I was lucky for not telling him about my video blog before starting it. Otherwise, he would have tried everything to talk me out of the idea because it sounded "incredibly stupid."

George Bernard Shaw famously said, "All great truths begin as blasphemies." And Mahatma Gandhi said: "First they ignore you, then they laugh at you, then they fight you, then you win."

The next time everyone accepts your idea or proposal without a hint of disagreement, you might want to stop for a moment and ponder if it is the result of conventional and group thinking. And if someone thinks your idea is "incredibly stupid," consider the possibility that you might be onto something. Perhaps the question we should ask about an idea is not "How do I avoid rejection?" but "Is my idea worthy of rejection?"

## CHARACTER BUILDING
### 100 DAYS OF REJECTION: GIVE A SIDEWALK SPEECH

It is often said that people fear public speaking more than they fear death. During my 100 Days of Rejection, I made plenty of speeches to a diverse set of audiences. As a result, I have come to fear public speaking far less than I did before; in fact, I quickly started enjoying it. I'd given speeches about my story at Tony Hsieh's conference and at the University of Texas. However, standing onstage, in front of an audience of people who had purposely gathered to sit and listen to what I had to say, was one thing. It was safe, familiar, and predictable. Public speaking outside of that contained environment was another matter.

But I wanted to push myself again, so I devised a rejection challenge guaranteed to tap into this same sense of fear to see whether I could overcome it. The plan was to go to a random city street and start giving a public speech on the sidewalk. My wife, Tracy, would accompany me and film my experience from across the street. I had no idea if people would stop and listen, jeer or boo me, or just think I was crazy.

I wouldn't say I was scared to death—but I was close. If

you asked me which of my rejection attempts was the most frightening of them all, it was this one.

At 7:20 P.M. one evening, I set up a chair on a busy Austin sidewalk and propped up two signs nearby. The first read PUBLIC STORYTELLING @7:30PM. STAY IF INTERESTED. The second said KEEP AUSTIN WEIRD—a slogan that Austinites use to celebrate the city's dynamic and liberal culture. (The sign was meant to lend me some sort of credibility, suggesting to others that I was trying to be weird, just like them.)

Tracy filmed the episode from the start. During those ten minutes of waiting, I looked like the shiest guy in school about to ask the most beautiful girl to the prom. My face was pale and my lips were shaking. Five minutes passed by, and so did countless people. A cyclist stopped and looked at my signs, cocked her head, then started pedaling again. A chocolate Lab being walked by his owner sniffed the signs, but his owner quickly pulled him away and kept on going.

Ten minutes went by, and not one person stopped. Without an audience, I was ready to pack up and go home. But then I changed my mind. *I've come this far*, I thought. *Rejected or not, why not just give the speech anyway and see what happens.* I looked at Tracy, who was patiently standing across the street, filming my anguish, and signaled to her to wait. Then I stood up.

I cleared my throat, and these words came out of my mouth: "Hi, everyone. I am going to tell my story now. You are welcome to listen." Then I started my speech: "It was a Sunday. It was pretty warm. A guy was sitting in his house. . . ." I told the story of me knocking on Scott's door with a soccer ball.

The more I spoke, the more an odd sense of calm engulfed me, washing away the gut-wrenching jitters. I tried to focus exclusively on my speech, my movement, and the next word that came out of my mouth. It was like a light switch had flipped on.

A few people looked at me and slowed their steps. Others stopped and stood there. Soon, I had an audience of six people—and none of them left once they started listening.

Over the next fifteen minutes, I told my story—from quitting my job and building a company to being rejected by the investor and embarking on my rejection journey, and all the things I had learned along the way. I ended with what would later become, during other speeches, my signature line: "Rejection is like chicken. It's yummy or yucky depending on how you cook it. We cannot let the fear of rejection cripple us."

When I was done, my audience of six gave me a cheer.

"Thank you for telling your story, that was nice!" a person said.

"That was fantastic! How do we find you?" another woman asked.

A sense of pride and satisfaction filled my heart. I had fought through my fear, stuck with my goal despite being rejected by countless passersby, and gone on with my speech anyway.

And it was good that I did, because a few weeks later I had a much bigger audience to speak in front of. Three thousand entrepreneurs, bloggers, and writers filled the beautifully built double-decker Arlene Schnitzer Concert Hall in

Portland, Oregon. The occasion was the third annual World Domination Summit, a dynamic event billed as "a gathering of creative, interesting people from all over the world." The summit's founder and chief organizer, Chris Guillebeau, is an entrepreneur, blogger, and *New York Times* bestselling author of *The $100 Startup*. His goal is to inspire people to follow their passions and pursue their dreams—a cause I strongly believe in. After learning about my Krispy Kreme donut experience, he'd asked me to come to Oregon to share my story at his conference.

Before the event started, I looked at the speaker list and shook my head. It was filled with bestselling authors, including Gretchen Rubin (*The Happiness Project*), Donald Miller (*Blue Like Jazz*), and Danielle LaPorte (*The Desire Map*). There were also well-known entrepreneurs like Andrew Warner (Mixergy) and Jonathan Fields (Good Life Project). And then there was Nancy Duarte, who made a career of teaching public speaking and even designed the presentation that Al Gore gives in his movie *An Inconvenient Truth*.

And then there was me, a failed entrepreneur turned video blogger who spent his days seeking out rejection. I couldn't help but be nervous.

Before my speech, I paced back and forth backstage, breathing heavily. The pressure to measure up to the other speakers was overwhelming. Moreover, I had never even seen an audience that large, let alone spoken in front of one.

An event volunteer saw how nervous I was and offered to teach me some stretching techniques to calm myself down. Then the director told me there were five minutes to go. I gulped. After checking my microphone, the guy in charge of equipment patted me on the back and said, "You'll be fine. You are the rejection guy."

His comment cut through my nervousness and grabbed my attention. *Hmm . . . that's right! I am the freaking rejection guy! While other people run away from rejection, I looked for it 100 times!* If I'd managed to give my speech to an empty audience on a busy Austin street, then why should I be scared by a supportive audience that had paid to be here?

"One minute!" the director shouted.

My breathing started to slow down. I even managed a small smile—the kind you might get right before checkmating your opponent, which in this case was my own fear. I realized I had a weapon that no one else had—a wealth of experience in overcoming rejection.

Then it was time. "Go, go, go!" the director shouted, like a squad leader pushing his soldiers to advance toward a hail of bullets.

I walked onto the stage and into the spotlight. Three thousand people waited for me to begin. I took a full five seconds, surveying the beautiful theater from left to right. But I didn't see people. Instead I visualized that busy street in Austin, before anyone had stopped to hear my speech. In that moment, I knew I would be fine.

"It was a warm, November afternoon . . ." I began.

Twenty-three and half minutes later, I walked off the stage to a standing ovation. I was over the moon. I started hugging and high-fiving the backstage volunteers. But the standing ovation didn't stop, so Chris Guillebeau called me back to the stage to say a few final words. Standing there, I felt overwhelmed by joy and gratitude. I thanked the audience for their support and encouragement, and Chris for his invitation. But in my mind, I also thanked all those people who had passed me by on the street in Austin. That experience had made me strong and fearless.

Turning rejection into a positive requires courage. It requires looking rejection in the face and seeing it for what it really is—an experience that can either hurt you or help you, depending on how you look at it. The difference is attitude. By default, rejection is painful. If you treat it as a setback, a soul crusher, or a reason to quit, then that's what it will be. But if you can find the courage to step back and look at it differently, what you'll find is remarkable. Because what you'll find is that there is no bad rejection anymore. If you look carefully, you will find your willow, and a lovely new village.

Rejection really is like chicken. It is yummy or yucky, depending on how you cook it.

## LESSONS

1. Motivation: Rejection can be used as one of the strongest motivations to fuel someone's fire for achievement.

2. Self-Improvement: By taking the motion out of rejection, one can use it as an effective way to improve an idea or product.

3. Worthiness: Sometimes it is good to be rejected, especially if public opinion is heavily influenced by

group and conventional thinking, and if the idea is radically creative.

4. Character Building: By seeking rejection in tough environments, one can build up the mental toughness to take on greater goals.

CHAPTER 10

# FINDING MEANING

**O**BVIOUSLY, THE REJECTIONS I SOUGHT THROUGHOUT my 100 Days of Rejection did not have life and death consequences. When I asked Jackie for customized donuts or asked Robert to speak over Costco's intercom, there was nothing on the line except my own internal battle with rejection. But I found myself wondering how it would feel to turn my efforts toward more meaningful questions. What lessons could I learn from the deepest rejections in life, when there was no upside in sight? What I found was that sometimes it's not about getting a yes or a no. Sometimes facing rejection is about something else. It's about being willing to endure rejection because there's a profound reason for doing so.

## 100 DAYS OF REJECTION: MAKE DC SMILE

During my rejection journey, I had the privilege of meeting many people on interesting journeys of their own. Massoud Adibpour was one of those people. After graduating from James Madison University in 2005, he joined a consulting firm in Washington, DC. The income was great—but Adibpour was miserable. The place lacked creativity, he told me, and while working there he felt like just a number. Eventually he quit and started traveling the world. After visiting far-flung places like Thailand and Cambodia, he returned to DC much happier and ready to simplify his life. Music had always been his passion, and soon he found his dream job as a concert promoter. But he also felt a profound urge to help make other people as happy as he was. So in 2013, he started a side project—or more like a mission, really—called Make DC Smile.

Every Monday morning, Adibpour holds big poster-size signs covered in positive messages at a busy DC street corner. He holds up the signs to passing traffic while waving and smiling. His only purpose, he says, is to "promote positivity and hopefully take people out of their negative element." His signs—and his smile—have become part of DC's Monday morning commuting landscape. They have also caught the attention of major news outlets, who seem fascinated by a man so determined to make others smile.

Adibpour heard about my 100 Days of Rejection project and reached out, hoping to collaborate with me in some way. I already had a trip planned to DC, so we agreed to meet up—and for me to join his campaign on my trip. In order to turn the experience into a rejection attempt, in addition to waving Adibpour's signs, we would ask strangers passing by to join us.

A few weeks later, on an unseasonably chilly morning, I met Adibpour at the base of the Washington Monument. A tall man sporting a beanie, he greeted me with a warm and genuine smile. After exchanging a handshake and then a bro-hug, we headed to our street corner and started waving signs at passing cars. In truth, I had no idea how Monday morning commuters would react to an Asian guy and a Middle Eastern guy holding up messages imploring them to be happy. This was DC, after all, a city known for its tough commute and even tougher people. I was ready for anything.

Adibpour had brought a stack of signs with him. We worked our way down his signage from HONK IF YOU LOVE SOMEONE to TODAY IS AWESOME to DON'T BE SO HARD ON YOURSELF—with mixed results. Some drivers honked in acknowledgment, waved at us, or actually smiled. The rest shot us confused looks or ignored us altogether.

After fifteen minutes of sign waving, we started asking pedestrians walking by to join us. We quickly experienced a barrage of rejections, mostly from well-dressed men and women hustling off to work (although one of them, after turning down our offer, added, "I love the signs"). A family of four, with the parents tightly holding the hands of their two young boys, hustled by without even slowing down. The parents looked determined not to acknowledge our existence, even though the kids seemed interested.

Eventually, a man who looked like a student approached us. His name was Peter. He was intrigued by what we were doing and volunteered to join in. After sifting through the signs, he finally settled on the one that simply said: SMILE. And with that, our happiness team expanded 50 percent. I instantly felt stronger and more motivated. Having a third person join us felt like a movement.

For a while, it seemed as though Peter would be the only one to hop in. Our efforts to recruit more people ended in a dizzying string of rejections. "How many rejections do you think we've gotten?" I asked Adibpour at one point, having lost count. He half jokingly replied it was maybe three hundred. "But it is good," he said, "because they were thinking about the signs." To him, that in itself was enough to be counted as a yes.

Soon after, a couple with a child wandered by, looking lost. Adibpour asked if they needed help getting somewhere. After giving them directions to the aquarium, he invited them to join us. "We are protesting against unhappiness," I added. All three of them laughed, picked up signs, and started waving them to the traffic. I'm not sure why they agreed to join, but they really got into it. We had doubled our team in size again, and it was a blast.

The Make DC Smile episode was a fun experience for sure, but once was enough for me. For Massoud Adibpour, it was a completely different story. His positive attitude and persistence were genuine and unrelenting. He never showed any disappointment or distress, even when we were getting rejected trying to recruit people to join. Wearing a seemingly permanent bright smile, he focused on showing me the right way to wave, the right signs to display, and the proper way to invite people to join us. His happy, calm energy was infectious.

By the time I met him, he had been waving his signs week after week for more than a year, through the hot summer and cold winter, with no monetary reward whatsoever. A bright and well-educated guy, he could have used his time to do something else, like taking on a second job or starting his own business. From a pure economics standpoint, I told him, Make DC Smile made no sense at all.

"You can't buy happiness," he replied, matter-of-factly.

Adibpour had quit his well-paying consulting job because he saw no meaning in it. But he had found meaning in the Make DC Smile project, and that sense of purpose seemed to inoculate him against the fact that he was constantly being rejected by strangers. "Rejection is a terrible feeling, especially when the weather is cold," he explained. "But I've gotten used to it. Not everyone smiles or acknowledges me. Gradually, as I made others happy, I became happier myself."

Adibpour's example demonstrated that happiness doesn't always come from money, comfort, or acceptance. That's why some of the most brilliant and influential people spend their time and effort on things that have only intrinsic reward. Mother Teresa didn't run a hedge fund, and Martin Luther King Jr. didn't go into real estate. Instead, they spent their lives advocating for causes that were meaningful to them, even though they lived through hardships and rejection.

## FINDING EMPATHY

The experiences I had standing on the street asking for different things—whether it was money or just attention—were some of the most difficult of my rejection journey. I felt I was constantly being judged by strangers based on the way I looked, the way I carried myself, and what I was asking for. When people lowered their heads to avoid eye contact or sped off without acknowledging my existence, it wasn't the most pleasant feeling.

These experiences also made me wonder about the real panhandlers I have encountered. They weren't trying to be noble or conducting social experiments. They were begging for money for themselves for reasons not known to me. In the sweltering heat or bitter cold, in clouds of exhaust and oceans of noise, through bullets of mockery and arrows of judgment, panhandling seemed like the worst job in the world.

There used to be a gigantic divide between my life and the lives of the panhandlers I used to pass every day on my own commutes through Austin. Even though we lived in the same city and breathed the same air, our worlds couldn't be further apart. But my own experiences with facing rejection on the street gave me an empathy for panhandlers that I never thought I would have. It also gave me the desire to get to know them and understand their world.

## 100 DAYS OF REJECTION: INTERVIEW A PANHANDLER

One day, as a rejection attempt, I approached a panhandler standing on a street corner next to a traffic light at the busy highway off-ramp and asked if I could interview him. I had no idea if he would agree. Would there be a conversation, or would this be another rejection?

He looked to be in his sixties and had a bushy white beard that instantly made me think of Santa Claus. He wore sunglasses and a baseball hat that read "Veteran." Military dog tags hung from his neck. He also had a big sign that read DISABLED VETERAN. There is no mistake in his message and identity.

His name was Frank. While he agreed to the interview, he also looked around uneasily, as if checking if he was in some kind of trouble.

In the next ten minutes, he told me his incredible story. Originally from Michigan, Frank fought in the Vietnam War but became injured and couldn't work. His brain injury also caused him to have a speech impediment, which made it difficult to understand him. He had been waiting for more than eighteen months for the government to upgrade his veteran disability benefit to cover more than just basic food and shelter, but it hadn't come yet.

Worst of all, Frank and his wife had a six-year-old son who was the size of a three-year-old due to a severe heart condition. He had an upcoming surgery scheduled at a Children's Hospital in Corpus Christi, a city 250 miles south of Austin. Frank was on the street panhandling so they could afford the trip, which would require him and his wife to stay in a hotel for up to two weeks. While insurance would cover the surgery, Frank simply didn't have the money to get himself there.

After we'd chatted for a while, I thanked Frank for sharing his story with me and gave him whatever cash I had. He graciously thanked me. He also made sure I knew how proud he was of his military service to his country. He asked me, "Have you ever served?" I said, "No, but I serve my wife." Frank gave me a hearty laugh, and for a moment I could see what he might look like in happier times. His smile made him look ten years younger.

After a handshake, Frank went back to his post, and I got back in my car with a heavy heart. Frank had faced so many kinds of rejection and misfortune. And now he was standing there, a proud and desperate father who once served and sacrificed for his country, being rejected by hundreds upon hundreds of drivers passing by. If only they knew Frank's story, they might actually stop. It might take him mere hours to get the funds he needed, not days or weeks or longer.

In a talk at the Royal Society for the Encouragement of Arts (RSA), University of Houston social researcher Brene Brown described the difference between sympathy and empathy: "Empathy fuels connection, while sympathy drives disconnection," she said. "Empathy is feeling with people. . . . When someone is in a deep hole and they shout out from the bottom and say 'I'm stuck, it's dark, I'm overwhelmed.' And then we look and we say 'Hey' and we climb down: 'I know what it's like down here, and you are not alone.' Sympathy is [someone saying from the top] 'Ooh! It's bad, huh? You want a sandwich?' "

I have sympathy toward many causes and situations, which often seem remote and out of my control. But now I have empathy toward panhandlers asking for money to help their families. I had no way to confirm what Frank told me. But to me, it didn't matter, because I knew how crappy it was to be on the street asking for money. In a way, I was grateful for the rejection I'd experienced when asking for money, because it gave me a chance to climb down into the deep hole Frank was in, just for a moment, to know what it was like.

Stephen Covey, the bestselling author of the book *The Seven Habits of Highly Effective People*, said: "When you show deep empathy toward others, their defensive energy goes down, and positive energy replaces it. That's when you can get more creative in solving problems." And Jack Welch, the former CEO of General Electric and a man widely considered to be one of the best business leaders of all time, said, "If you have everything else you need in terms of talent and skill, your humanity will come to be your most appealing virtue to an organization." Any rejection can be an opportunity for empathy if you look at it the right way. We can allow rejection to shut us down, but we can also allow it to open us up, to compel us to understand and help others.

## FINDING VALUE

### 100 DAYS OF REJECTION: INTERVIEW A
### FEMALE BODYBUILDER

Like I mentioned earlier, throughout my 100 Days I received a lot of requests from people, and some of those requests were pretty off the wall. One of the strangest I received was from John, a forty-nine-year-old casino dealer from California. More than anything, John wanted me to interview a female bodybuilder.

The request itself was unusual to say the least—but so was John's persistence. When he first sent me the request, I dismissed the idea as bizarre and as something that didn't fit my personality or my interests. I also didn't find his request that challenging. Why would I be afraid to ask a bodybuilder for an interview? And an interview for what? I wasn't even sure if he was serious or joking. So I ignored it. Then he sent me the request again—and again, and again. He even sent me videos of female bodybuilders performing in contests, trying to convince me of their beauty. By the twentieth time, I started to get curious—not about his request or female bodybuilding, but about his tenacity and reasoning. So I wrote back and asked him why he wanted me to do this so badly.

It turned out that John had always been fascinated by female bodybuilders. He wanted to find out why they enter a field dominated by men, and how they value beauty. He had tried to approach a couple of bodybuilders himself and was blown off, so he developed this crippling fear of rejection from the very people he most admired. It was to a point that he just had to ask me to fulfill the wish for him.

His story made his request make more sense, but I still didn't know how to fit this interview into my rejection journey, so I politely said no.

But John didn't give up. He kept going and going. Each time I posted a new video, he would follow up with encouragement in the comment area, but also beg me to interview a female bodybuilder, explaining how much it would mean to him.

I said earlier that every rejection has a number. For John, that number was forty-four. After his forty-fourth ask, I finally gave in and said yes. After all, it's hard to say no to something this important to a loyal fan.

Through LinkedIn, I sent out messages to three female bodybuilders in the Austin area, requesting a sit-down interview. One of them said yes. Her name was Melanie Daly. She was an Austinite who owned a small but successful personal coaching gym and had won multiple gold medals in national natural bodybuilding contests.

In the interview, Melanie answered all John's questions, some of which were rather personal. She talked about why she became a bodybuilder and what drove her to be excellent in her profession.

Melanie also revealed an unexpected fact about her profession. Bodybuilders as a group have to confront their own rejection fear on a constant basis. They are afraid of both their own rejection and that from others. Because they put enormous amounts of work and time into their own bodies, she said, they tend to be haunted by imperfections and are very insecure about themselves. They often reject themselves.

Moreover, female bodybuilders often feel rejected by society. When people think about feminine beauty, the images that pop up usually don't involve large muscles and pumping iron. Because Melanie and her fellow bodybuilders view beauty and health differently from the rest of the society, they face judgment and rejection—especially in the dating world—every day.

In that respect, John had more in common with the people he so admired than he even realized.

John's persistence had got me wondering: What would I be willing to go through forty rejections for? Or four hundred rejections? Or four thousand rejections? Maybe for a good deal on a car, or for a successful business or career. Definitely for a great marriage and for the well-being of my loved ones. The higher the number went, the more valuable the things I was willing to be rejected for became. When it came to love, friendship, and health, though, I realized that the number approached infinity.

When you don't know how much you want and value something, rejection can become almost a measuring stick. Some of the most successful people obtained their achievements *only* after going through the most gut-wrenching rejection. Because it was through that rejection that they discovered how much pain they were willing to experience in order to obtain their goal.

Comedian Louis C.K. decided he wanted to become a comedy writer and stand-up performer as a kid growing up in Boston. Possessing a rare combination of brazenness and heart, disrespectfulness and relatability, crudeness and insight, Louis C.K. blossomed into his life dream. By his midforties, he had accomplished more than most comedians could ever hope for.

As a stand-up performer, he frequently performed on the most popular late-night TV shows, and his tours usually sold out within hours. His one-hour specials were made into DVDs that yielded millions in profit, and he even had his own show on HBO. He's been nominated for thirty Emmy Awards, winning five.

Given his innate talent and the fact that he had managed to achieve his dream career, you might think Louis C.K.'s success was the natural outcome of all the right lucky breaks. Yet that couldn't be further from reality. In fact, he was rejected over and over again in the pursuit of his dream. And it was *because* of all those rejections that he found out how badly he wanted a career in comedy.

When he was seventeen, Louis C.K. gave his first stand-up performance during an open mic night at a Boston night club where aspiring comedians would get onstage to tell jokes. The audiences at these events are notoriously tough on people, often booing them off the stage. It's a nerve-racking way for people with stand-up dreams to test their talent, and an equally convenient way for them to give up their dreams after public rejection.

Not knowing anything about the setting nor having ever even attempted stand-up, Louis C.K. spent days preparing two hours' worth of material that he thought was great. But the audience thought differently.

After only about a minute and a half, "the people just

stared at me," he recalled in an interview about his career on the *Howard Stern Show*. After delivering a joke that clearly bombed horribly, he'd said, "I think that's all I really have," and walked off the stage, humiliated. The emcee proceeded to make fun of him for ten minutes afterward. "It was a terrible feeling, and I wanted to die," Louis C.K. said.

But he gathered up the courage to try again. A famous local comic put him in front of a bigger crowd without any preparation. "It was awful," Louis C.K. recalled. "Literally my hands were shaking, and my heart was pounding so that my head kept bobbling up and down." Needless to say, this time it went even worse and he bombed again.

These thrown-to-the-wolves experiences would have led many young dreamers to believe they didn't have the talent or that the career they dreamed of wasn't as glamorous as they had imagined. In the popular "fail fast" culture that many entrepreneurs and businesses now are clinging to, most, if not all, would have concluded that doing stand-up comedy might not be their thing. Most of them would have moved on to try something else, perhaps something that didn't involve such public exposure.

When asked why didn't he walk away at that point, Louis C.K. explained: "A little time went by and I was like, well, I didn't die, and I am still interested. That felt bad when it was going on, and I'm healed now, and I'm still interested in trying again. I made it through the bad feeling. I can handle feeling that bad."

He toiled away in Boston night club obscurity for eight years, struggling to make ends meet. Many nights he was re-

quired to perform to literally empty rooms at clubs, because
in case someone walked in, there would be a show.

One night, Jim Downey, the director of *Saturday Night
Live*—which has always been a life-changing and dream platform for comedians—came to town looking for fresh writer
talent. He selected every single comic who auditioned—
*except* Louis C.K. It was like the world was giving him the
clearest possible message to quit. But Louis C.K. still didn't
give up. The rejections, in fact, were a real gut check. He'd
been rejected in a pretty dramatic way, but he still didn't
want to give up. This realization gave him the strength to
pursue comedy despite these early experiences. Later, his
"lucky" break finally came when he was discovered by Conan
O'Brien and got a job as a writer. The rest is history. But
when you think about the trajectory of his journey, Louis
C.K.'s "lucky break" wasn't really luck at all. It was the result
of being able to endure multiple devastating rejections over a
long period of time.

Most of us grew up harboring big dreams, whether it was
becoming the president of the United States or being a rocket
scientist or doing stand-up comedy for a living. Yet most of
us abandon these early dreams. As we get older, we learn
through self-reflection that we don't really have the combination of passion, drive, or talent for that particular dream.
Or we learn through rejection that the world isn't receptive
to our endeavors. So we change course, often finding success
in other professions. Again, this is the "Upside of Quitting"
that economist authors Stephen Dubner and Steven Levitt
talk about.

But some people don't give up—even after the world initially, or even repeatedly, rejects them. They become who they always wanted to become because, through the worst rejections, they learned how much their dreams mean to them.

Dostoevsky once said, "The only thing I dread [is] not to be worthy of my sufferings." The same goes for rejection. Is your dream bigger than your rejections? If it is, maybe it's time to keep going, instead of giving up.

## FINDING MISSION

Most of the time, when we talk about rejection, we're talking about one person or one group saying no to another. But sometimes life events are so profound and life changing that they make people feel rejected by fate, or even by God. How does a person find meaning when his or her world turns upside down—or, in the case of Major Scotty Smiley, literally pitch-black?

Many of my classmates at Duke Business School were incredibly intelligent and creative. Some went on to become successful business leaders and entrepreneurs. Yet if you ask me which classmate left the biggest impression and impact on me, it would be Scotty Smiley.

Smiley was a U.S. Army first lieutenant at the time and had served in Iraq. On April 6, 2005, his platoon spotted a suspicious vehicle with a single male driver heading toward their post. Smiley was the closest to the vehicle and fired a warning shot, but the driver didn't stop. Lieutenant Smiley had a decision to make. He could aim at the driver and stop him with a bullet, or fire another warning shot, attempting to spare the driver's life. He decided, fatefully, on the latter. Smiley remembers seeing the driver look toward him, then a second later detonate a suicide car bomb. Smiley was much closer to the vehicle than the rest of his platoon—he'd purposely tried to stop the vehicle before it got closer to his men—so the bomb didn't hurt anyone except Smiley.

The next thing Smiley remembered was lying in the hospital. Some shrapnel had penetrated his left eye and gone into his brain, and the doctor told him he would never see again.

Smiley told us this story during our school commencement. "It is often said man's greatest fear is to go blind," he said. "I met that fear that day."

A deeply religious man, Smiley felt rejected by God. Why had God taken away his sight and left him blind for life? His life went into a tailspin. "My life, in my opinion, was taken from me," he told Fox News during an interview about his experiences. "It's hard for anyone to deal with that. Denial, anger, resentment, fear . . . I didn't know what to think."

He was also afraid of being rejected by the army, which had become the bedrock of his life and his career. In almost all cases, such debilitating injury would mean leaving active duty.

But Smiley wasn't willing to settle for that fate. He wanted to go on with his life and live it to the fullest—*inside* the army. He told our class: "I didn't want to be Lt. Dan Taylor"—the fictional character in the movie *Forrest Gump* who becomes overly bitter after losing his leg in the Vietnam War.

So Smiley preempted the army's inevitable decision by making one of his own. Instead of quietly retiring from the army, he petitioned to stay in, taking on jobs to help and inspire other injured soldiers. The army agreed, and Smiley became the army's first blind active-duty officer.

In the meantime, he climbed Mount Rainier, skied in Colorado, surfed in Hawaii, skydived, and completed a triathlon. He received a Purple Heart and a Bronze Star from the army. He then won an ESPY award as the world's Best Outdoor Athlete in 2008. After graduating from Duke's MBA program, he went on to teach a leadership course at West Point, then became the commander of the Warrior Transition Unit at West Point's medical center. Recently, he received the army's prestigious MacArthur Leadership Award and was promoted to major. He also became an author of the book *Hope Unseen*, telling his story.

Smiley's deep faith never again wavered. It became his mission to use his story to inspire millions of soldiers, athletes, churchgoers, and everyday people to shift their perspectives on what "rejection" means and how to turn adverse circumstances into strength, motivation, and mission in life.

To this day, Scotty Smiley's story continues to inspire me. I sat in the same classroom with him for my entire first year at school. Other than using special software for blind people that would read homework and course material to him, he participated just like everyone else. I remember one day after class I helped him to walk to the front of the school building where his family was waiting for him. He hugged his beautiful and loving wife, Tiffany, and picked up and kissed his toddler son, and waved good-bye to me.

I usually feel great sympathy toward those with disabilities. But in that moment, I realized there is no way I could feel bad for Scotty Smiley. I thought to myself, *My God, what a guy! And what a privilege it is for me to know this man!*

Losing his eyesight was a tragedy. But instead of being defined by tragedy like so many others, Scotty decided to define himself through his reaction. In a way, he found his new mission in life through his rejection and turned a story of tragedy into one filled with meaning and joy. Because he chose to.

In a way, these stories remind me of a much more grim yet profound one: the story of Dr. Viktor Frankl. I read Frankl's book *Man's Search for Meaning* many years ago, and its message has always stuck with me. The book describes the time he was forced to spend in Nazi concentration camps. He and his fellow prisoners were stripped of everything that was once valuable to them—from comfort and security to human dignity and justice. Many times, life and death were decided randomly, based on the whims and moods of sadistic guards. However, Frankl still discovered one thing in the experience that no one thought was possible: meaning.

Frankl found that even through the deepest suffering and absence of physical freedom he could find meaning in his condition, whether it was to strengthen himself spiritually or to help care for other prisoners. Having meaning not only prevented him from losing hope and ending his own life, but it also gave him the freedom to choose what type of attitude he exhibited toward it all.

We might not have freedom to control our situations, but we have freedom to find meaning in every experience, even when it's rejection, whether it's empathy, value, or a new mission in life.

## LESSONS

1.  Find Empathy: All rejections are shared by many people in the world. One can use rejection and suffering to obtain empathy and understanding of other people.

2.  Find Value: Repeated rejections can serve as the measuring stick for one's resolve and belief. Some of the greatest triumphant stories come only after gutwrenching rejections.

3.  Find Mission: Sometimes the most brutal rejections in life signal a new beginning and mission for the rejectee.

CHAPTER 11

# FINDING FREEDOM

**I**T'S BEEN SAID THAT NO ONE CAPTURED MORE EARTHLY glory than Alexander the Great during his reign as the emperor of Macedon. Undefeated in battle, Alexander conquered territory stretching from Eastern Europe to North Africa to South Asia. His presence struck fear in the hearts of every man he encountered—except one.

One day, when Alexander's army was crossing the Indus River into India, he encountered a man sitting in the woods, naked and in a lotus position, staring at the sky. The man was known as the gymnosophist, or the "naked philosopher." Puzzled, Alexander asked him what he was doing. The gymnosophist answered: "I'm experiencing nothingness. What are *you* doing?" Alexander replied: "I'm conquering the world." Then they both laughed at each other's foolishness.*

* Story source: "East vs. West—The Myths That Mystify" by Devdutt Pattanaik at TED India, November 2009.

Alexander and the gymnosophist couldn't understand each other because they lived in different paradigms. Alexander, who was trained in Aristotle's linear Greek philosophy and believed in spectacular achievement in his one and only life, thought the gymnosophist was wasting his time by sitting there and doing nothing. The gymnosophist, on the other hand, held the asceticism belief that life's true meaning comes from abstinence from worldly pleasures. He thought Alexander was wasting *his* time by conquering the world, which to the gymnosophist meant little in the grand scheme of things.

Yet Alexander the Great and the Indian gymnosophist were in fact both conquering the world. Alexander was conquering the collective and objective world that we all live in, and the gymnosophist was conquering the individual and subjective world only he lived in. Throughout history, mankind has been striving to discover and conquer both of these worlds. In fact, it's at the point where the inner and outer worlds intersect that many of the most amazing and profound philosophical, religious, and artistic breakthroughs occur.

I started my rejection journey with a very straightforward goal: to overcome rejection so that I could become free to take more risks in my business and in my career. Put another way, I was focusing on the outer world and how to get better at dealing with it. But in the end, the biggest surprise of my journey was how much overcoming rejection would change my inner world—the way that I experience both the world and myself. Inside, I have found a sense of freedom and peace. And I had no idea how much mental and psycho-

logical bondage had enslaved me until I was able to elimi-
nate it.

## FREEDOM TO ASK
### 100 DAYS OF REJECTION: FLY A PLANE

By the time I neared the end of my rejection journey, I was
regularly getting far more yeses than nos. When I asked a
stranger on the street to play rock-paper-scissors-lizard-
Spock—a wacky expansion of the classic game rock-paper-
scissors—he went for it immediately. The next day, I visited
the fast-food restaurant Sonic, where employees wear roller
skates to serve food to customers waiting in their cars. I
asked if I could borrow a pair of skates to have some fun
on my own. They asked me to sign a waiver, and off I went.
For my next attempt, I saw a construction crew operating
a bucket truck that was fixing a business sign on top of a
building. I asked them if I could ride in it, and they put me in
the bucket, lifting me fifty feet above the ground and swing-
ing me around just for thrills.

I was having a lot of fun doing all this cool and wacky
stuff, but I was also a little frustrated with all the yeses. I
wasn't sure whether I'd become so good at asking for things
that people had a hard time turning me down, or whether
my requests were too easy. As strange as it might sound, I
really wanted more rejections to achieve some balance in my
learning. So I decided to come up with a rejection attempt
that there was no way anyone would let me do.

For rejection attempt number 92, I visited a local airport
and I asked a pilot named Desmond if he would let me fly

his plane. I had no license, no experience, and honestly, no courage to fly a plane. I simply asked so I could get rejected.

But Desmond said yes.

It turned out he owned what's called a gyroplane—a type of small, unenclosed rotorcraft that looks like a miniature version of a helicopter and can take off and land with ease. To me, it resembled more of a motorcycle than an airplane.

In fact, Desmond was a gyroplane enthusiast who couldn't wait to tell people about how awesome his aircraft was. What I thought was a crazy request was actually an opportunity for Desmond to share something he loved.

To make sure I wouldn't crash and die, he went up with me, teaching me how to fly it. It was a far cry from the gigantic commercial jets I was accustomed to. And precisely for that reason, I learned what real flying was, and perhaps how the Wright brothers and early pilots felt when they were in the air.

Before that day, when I thought of flying, I thought of standing in long frustrating lines, taking off my belt and shoes while making sure my pants didn't drop, walking through the body scanner wondering if it would give me cancer someday, sitting on dirty carpet charging my mobile phone while waiting out a flight delay, fighting for overhead luggage space and elbow room with the guy sitting next to me once we boarded, and longingly peeking out the plane's little windows to get a glimpse of the sky.

But in the gyroplane, I felt like a bird. No wonder Desmond loved it so much! He taught me to turn, to glide, and to climb higher in the sky. We did 360s, nosedives, and sharp turns. One minute I was two feet above a cornfield, just like a seagull skimming above the ocean. The next minute I was a thousand feet in the sky, just like an eagle.

It was the best flight of my life.

After we landed, I was consumed with one thought: *What if I had never asked Desmond if I could fly his plane in the first place? I would have missed this whole experience. I wouldn't even know gyroplanes existed.*

Looking back over my 100 Days of Rejection, had I not asked, there were so many experiences I would not have had, from the silly to the profound: the Olympic donuts, having a talk-show host sing to my son on national TV, learning to be a greeter and a panhandler, becoming a professor and an office manager for a day, touring a fire station and a hotel, buying a McGriddles in the afternoon, assembling a smile-giving team in Washington, DC, giving a speech on the street, and learning more about the profession of female bodybuilding than I ever thought I would. I have so many incredible memories I would never have formed. These experiences wouldn't have occurred if I hadn't sought them out—they existed only because I had asked.

Yes, I learned to make my requests in more artistic and scientific ways, and to maneuver around rejection when it came. And yes, I still got rejected. Everyone who sets out on this journey will get rejected somewhere along the way. But by not even asking, we are rejecting ourselves by default—and probably missing out on opportunity as a result. A 2011 study by the consulting firm Accenture found that less than half of working Americans (44 percent of women and

48 percent of men) have *ever* asked for a raise. Yet statistically, 85 percent of those who ask for a raise get something.

My son, Brian, who is one and half years old now, never hesitates to ask me for things. His finger is like a magic wand, pointing to anything that he wants. Although he might get a rejection from me, he is never afraid to ask. I am sure I was the same way as a child, and we were all the same way at one point in our lives.

But as we grow older and "wise up," we learn that we can't always get what we want and that sometimes we need to be judicious in making requests. And sure, constantly asking for $100 from your friend might not be a good idea and you might quickly run out of friends. However, we let the pendulum of requests swing too far in the direction of not asking for what we want due to fear of rejection. We stop making requests to the detriment of our dreams, aspirations, and relationships. We start to get overly timid and careful, and we start to tell ourselves stories about how we shouldn't bother people, how we would get rejected anyway, and how we will someday ask "when the timing is right," even though the "right timing" never comes. We tell ourselves all these lies because of one thing: we want to avoid rejection.

My 100 Days of Rejection helped me shed all that I'd learned about fearing rejection and returned me to a much earlier state, the very state that my son, Brian, is in right now. I feel I can ask for anything I want or need and not be afraid of rejection, judgment, and disapproval. I've learned that amazing things can happen when I reach out and take that first step—and my excitement about those possibilities has begun to overshadow any fear I have about potential rejection. In a way, I am not afraid of people anymore, and I have never felt that way before in my life.

## FREEDOM TO ACCEPT YOURSELF

When you are not afraid anymore, that attitude will start to manifest in your personal relationships. Remember my uncle, the one whose dismissal of my idea to invent a shoe-skate hybrid back in college paralyzed my entrepreneurial drive? I haven't always agreed with him, but I know my uncle has always loved and cared for me like his own son. And he has always wanted the best for me, in terms of both achieving financial success and pursuing my dreams. But he has a different perspective on how I should get there. More than anything, our differences are generational.

My uncle is a baby boomer who grew up in China. He later migrated to the United States with very little money. He worked very hard, step by step, to achieve his goals. Eventually, he fulfilled his dream of going to law school and established a very successful legal practice. To him, becoming a lawyer was like achieving the American dream. It also made him financially independent, which he to this day believes should be the number one goal of any young person.

I, on the other hand, a quintessential millennial, didn't grow up wanting to be rich; I grew up wanting to be the next Bill Gates, and there was a clear distinction. While Bill Gates was rich for sure, he also changed the world and helped launch the computer revolution that made much of today's information technology possible. It was the changing-the-world-and-making-it-better part that attracted me deeply.

That's why I dreamed of becoming an entrepreneur and loathed being just another cog in a corporate machine, no matter how much I was paid.

Over the course of the past decade, I came to believe that this difference between us was probably the reason my uncle flat out rejected my wheels-on-shoes start-up idea. He thought entrepreneurship and start-ups were dreamy fantasies and that instead I should be climbing a corporate ladder or getting a professional degree so that I could make tons of money.

But was his rejection really due to our generational value differences? My 100 Days of Rejection taught me how dangerous it is to make assumptions about another person's thoughts and motives (remember the hairdresser!). My uncle's rejection had happened more than a decade earlier, but I had never asked him to explain to me what had been going through his mind. I had just assumed it was because uncle thought I was daydreaming.

So I called him. Believe me, making that phone call wasn't easy. In fact, it was very uncomfortable. However, I told myself that if I could ask an auditorium filled with people to listen to me speak, then surely I could ask my uncle why he'd rejected my idea. I mustered all the swagger and calm I've learned through rejection therapy just to dial his number.

I could tell he was a little surprised by my question. "Well," he said after a short pause, "I didn't like the idea. I thought it wouldn't work."

"Wait . . . hold on," I said. "It wasn't because you thought being an entrepreneur was dreamy and dumb?"

"No," he replied in a matter-of-fact tone. "I have always liked the fact that you think big. Sometimes it's unrealistic, but you dared to dream and that was good. But the idea was just not good, in my opinion."

Hearing this from him, I felt both relieved and a little stupid. For the longest time, I thought my uncle rejected me out of principle—that he thought I had my head in the clouds, that I didn't have what it took to run a successful start-up, that I was being irresponsible and unrealistic. I had carried those fears with me for a long time. But I was wrong. He rejected me because he wasn't sold on the specific idea that I had brought to him. Had the idea been something he liked or even understood, he would have gladly said yes.

At that moment, I wished I could have done my 100 Days of Rejection as a young man rather than as an adult. Maybe if there had been a course called Rejection Training or Rejection 101 in college, I would have learned all the principles by now. I would not have misunderstood this rejection and let it affect me so deeply. It might have even put my life on another route. Maybe, instead of Roger Adams inventing Heelys, I would have been the first to realize the idea.

Had I known then what I know now, I would have dealt with this rejection very differently. In fact, I made a list of the most important lessons I've learned about rejection so that I can keep myself from ever falling into bad habits.

**Rejection is human.** Neither rejection nor acceptance is the objective truth about the merit of an idea or even a product. In my case, I mistook my uncle's word for truth and thus gave up way too early.

**Rejection is an opinion.** It reflects the rejector more than the rejectee. In my uncle's opinion, I was a good ideas person, but this particular idea wouldn't work. As a lawyer, he was no guru of consumer products—he wasn't well versed in the world of the potential customer for the shoes. But his opinion was far from definitively right. Even if he had been a product genius like Steve Jobs, he still could have been wrong about the idea, like Steve Jobs was wrong plenty of times in his career.

**Rejection has a number.** I could have asked a lot more people about the idea than just my uncle. Judging by Heelys's success, odds are that someone I talked to would have liked the idea, which would have given me the encouragement I'd needed to pursue my idea to the next step.

**Ask "why" before good-bye.** If we had had this "why" conversation in the moment rather than years later, who knows what could have happened? Instead, I let pain dictate my response and went into an emotional shell. I didn't find out the true reason for my uncle's rejection until now.

**Retreat, don't run.** I could have retreated and pitched my idea to him in a different way, such as building a model by inserting wheels into real shoes and seeing what he thought of that. Instead, I ran senselessly like a scared soldier after a bloody rout.

**Collaborate, don't contend.** I could have turned my uncle into a collaborator by asking him to imagine how he, or his kids, might use an invention like the one I was proposing. Getting him to envision my idea in a real-world setting might have shown him that I was onto something, after all.

**Switch up, don't give up.** My goal was to become an

entrepreneur, not a one-idea man. I could have "switched it up" by coming back to him with an entirely different invention idea instead of giving it up altogether.

**Motivation.** I could have used the rejection as a motivation tool, pursuing the idea anyway and demonstrating to my uncle that I was up to the task, and that his rejection was wrong. I know that he, just like a loving father, would have been happy to be proven wrong by my success.

**Self-improvement.** I could have used his rejection to keep improving on my original blueprint, drawing a better and more practical model and sending it to him for further opinion.

**Worthiness.** I could have drawn the conclusion that the rejection possibly signaled the unconventional and creative nature of my idea.

**Character building.** Last, I could have used the no to strengthen instead of weaken myself mentally. A rejection from a family member is great preparation for rejection from future customers and investors. I could have said to myself: *If I didn't give up when my uncle said no, why would I give up when anyone else said no?*

Most important, I would have realized that rejection is nothing to be afraid of.

When it came to my shoes-with-wheels, I had gone with the worst option—letting a single rejection stop me from pursuing an idea simply because someone I loved and respected thought it didn't stack up.

Why did I have to ask my uncle for his approval in the first place? At the time, I sought acceptance, approval, and confirmation for seemingly everything, whether it was as big as a career choice or as small as what to eat. The sounds of "yes," "go ahead," "I agree," and "great idea" were like a drug to me, even in situations where I could easily make the decision myself.

The thousands of letters I received during my rejection journey tell me that approval-seeking isn't just my problem—it's more like an epidemic. Maybe it's the ways we're brought up as children, where conforming to our parents' wishes brings approval and praise and deviating from them means scolding and rejection. Or maybe it's the way we feel pressured to get others to like and accept us in our social circles or in the professional world. Or maybe it's the hardwired genetic tendencies to crave approval and fear rejection passed down from our ancestors. Whatever the source, constant approval-seeking causes us to bend ourselves in ways that are not authentic. We feel compelled to put on a façade to appear happy, competent, sophisticated, and worthy so we might be accepted by other people. Then, as we act and conform in different ways, over the long haul, we become someone very different from whom we were meant to be. We lose the inner child that grew up wanting to be the president, the rocket scientist, the artist, the musician, or the next Bill Gates.

In the end, what we really need is not acceptance from others but acceptance from ourselves. In fact, being comfortable with who we are should be a prerequisite—not the result—of seeking others' approval. We should all have the knowledge that who we are is good enough to get a yes from ourselves.

## LESSONS

1.  Freedom to Ask: We often deprive ourselves of the freedom to ask for what we want in fear of rejection and judgment. But amazing things often happen only after we take the first step.

2.  Freedom to Accept Yourself: Our inner need for approval-seeking forces us to constantly look for acceptance from other people. Yet the people from whom we need acceptance the most is ourselves.

CHAPTER 12

# FINDING POWER

**D**ISCOVERING A NEW INNER FREEDOM FROM REJECTION
was a big part of my 100 Days of Rejection. But I
had to do more than that—I also needed action. After all,
I dreamed of becoming an entrepreneur, not a philosopher
or self-improvement guru. And not just an entrepreneur,
but one whose work makes the world a better place in some
way. So what was also amazing to me was how the principles I learned could help me to achieve my outer world goals
as well.

## 100 DAYS OF REJECTION—BE THE WORST SALESMAN

The South By Southwest Conference is a massive music, film,
and technology event that takes over downtown Austin for

more than a week every year. Thousands of technology start-ups converge to promote their websites, their inventions, and their apps. Everyone brings out their best sales techniques, drenching you with their enthusiasm, persuasion, and bags of goodies.

I wondered what would happen if I tried to be the worst salesman, sounding confident but making absolutely no effort to persuade anyone to buy what I was pitching. How would people perceive a guy who was totally neutral if not clueless about what he was selling?

Wandering around the Austin Convention Center, I spotted two college-age women sitting in a corner of the room, holding a bunch of pamphlets and looking bored and hesitant. Their slumped demeanor suggested they had little confidence or interest in what they were selling. They were students at the University of Texas, they told me. They'd been hired by a start-up to hand out the pamphlets, explain the company's technology, and urge everyone to sign up for it on its website. When I asked if they had extra pamphlets so I could help hand them out, their faces lit up. They couldn't have been happier with my offer.

With a bunch of pamphlets in hand, I started my "terrible salesman" experiment. I approached random strangers who were either waiting to attend their next event or resting from a day of event hopping. I started each conversation by saying, "Can I promote something to you?" Then I told them I'd just picked up the pamphlets from other promoters and had no idea how good the product was. I also told them I had no vested interest in them taking a pamphlet or visiting the

company's website. Still, I made sure I sounded very confident, stood up straight, maintained eye contact, and gave a
big smile. I was friendly, relaxed, and not pushy.

People's responses were all over the board. One guy laughed
me off without taking a pamphlet, and another woman gave
me an "uh, sure"—a fake yes uttered probably just to get rid
of me. Someone else asked me how to use the product, and
I had to figure out an answer along with him since I had no
clue. One woman, an entrepreneur promoting a similar technology, said that what I was promoting basically did the same
thing as her own product. She immediately started to exam-
ine the company's website and compare it to hers, strategizing
on how to beat it. Incredibly, another woman grabbed hold
of the pamphlet and told me what I was offering was exactly
what she needed and had been looking for. She typed the address into her laptop, quickly scanned through the website,
and gave an excited "Right on!" It was as if I just delivered hot
pizza to a person who had been starving for days.

All in all, I offered pamphlets to ten strangers. Five people took them, two started to sign up in front of me, and the
other three rejected my offer.

Two things about this rejection attempt fascinated me.

First, I experienced a side of sales I hadn't known before.
I used to view sales strictly as a skill of persuasion. Getting
a yes or a no depended heavily on my communication skills.
But here I was, trying to be the worst salesperson, not knowing anything about the product and not caring about making
the sale. Some couldn't walk away quick enough, but others
engaged with me anyway because they had a need for or an

interest in the product. It reinforced that acceptance and rejection depend primarily on the other person's situation.

It also changed my perspective on marketing and sales. The egotistical notion that sales success is based purely on the strength of the salesperson—instead of the strength of the fit between the customer and what's being offered—now made no sense. In that way, rejection in sales is a *good* thing because it weeds out people who don't need or want my service. There is a saying that a good salesperson can sell ice cubes to Eskimos. But why not focus on finding the people stuck in one-hundred-degree heat dying for some relief? Or if we had to sell ice to Eskimos, why not find the ones who are vacationing on the streets of Las Vegas? They would appreciate it a lot more than those living in Canada and Alaska.

The second thing I observed was about myself. Because I was detached from the outcome and didn't feel the pressure to persuade or please, I could be 100 percent honest and say whatever I wanted. I was full of confidence. Most important, I had fun. And I actually think that some people picked up on the good spirits I was in and responded to that.

The people I approached had most likely been bombarded by many promoters throughout the day, each offering a rehearsed pitch or uninvited small talk. By just telling them that I was promoting something, I didn't beat around the bush and made my intention clear as the day. I bet no other salespeople started their conversation that way. That honesty felt refreshing to me, and I think to the people I approached as well. It even felt refreshing to people who watched the video of my sales attempt on my blog:

"'Can I promote something to you?' Just made my day.
Pure honesty. Awesome."—TheReinmira

"This could be a whole new marketing strategy :D"—
Irrational Action

Of course I am not some sort of sales guru who is discovering a new principle. Though I do believe that instead of focusing on learning sales techniques, if I can conquer fear first and start having fun, then everything, including using other sales techniques, would become much easier.

## DETACHMENT FROM RESULTS

Buddhism, Hinduism, and a host of other religions and philosophies promote the concept of detachment—of not taking anything that happens or doesn't happen personally. In Karma Yoga, the scripture Bhagavad Gita says that "by working without attachment one attains the Supreme." In *Tao Te Ching*, Lao Tzu wrote: "Care about people's approval and you will be their prisoner. Do your work, then step back, the only path to serenity." In his book *The Success Principles*, author Jack Canfield, creator of the Chicken Soup for the Soul series of books, urges readers to "live with high intention and low attachment."

Detachment shouldn't necessarily be from your passion or your ideas, but it does help to detach yourself from the results and the possibility of rejection. Yet detachment from results isn't something that most of us do well or even advocate. In society and in business, getting results—especially short-term or instant results—seems to be the only thing many people care about and measure themselves against. Salespeople measure their success by the number of sales they make against other salespeople. CEOs are judged by the next quarterly earnings report. Scientists are judged by the number of publications they write. According to a LinkedIn study on what its users put on their online profiles, "results oriented" is one of the most common buzzwords people use, because they believe it's what employers value the most. And they're often right.

I've learned that being solely "results oriented" is more than shortsighted. It actually leads to worse results in the long run because it leaves you unprepared to get feedback that might help you along your way. During my journey, I started to see a clear distinction between things I could control and things I couldn't. At first, I worried about the things I couldn't control, such as people's reactions and their perceptions of me. I would be extremely nervous and often gave out negative energy. Later on, when I started to give my full focus to what I could control, such as making eye contact, asking "why," listening, not running after a no, I found myself becoming more effective and confident in everything I did. I became more fearless in approaching strangers and venturing into the unknown.

John Wooden, the legendary basketball coach who took UCLA to a record ten NCAA championships in a span of eleven years, never mentioned winning and losing to his team. If there was anyone who knew about winning, it was he. Yet his measurement of success for his players was effort based, not results based. It was whether they had prepared thoroughly and played their best game, not beaten their opponent. That's what my rejection journey taught me: to play my best, and not worry about the results—even when the stakes seem impossibly high.

## 100 DAYS OF REJECTION—FROM INTERVIEWING OBAMA TO FINDING GOOGLE

Toward the end of my 100 Days journey, I felt some pressure to finish on a high note. Hundreds of people asked me what I would do for my hundredth request. "I don't know," I'd reply. "Hang out with Oprah?" I really wasn't sure. By that point, I felt fearless. Because I didn't care about the results, I was willing to ask for anything out of anybody at any time. Still, I wanted my hundredth request to be epic.

So I started a list of ideas. Here is a sample:

> I could ask to chat with Oprah or try to get on a popular talk show like *Ellen*.
> I could ask to interview or play basketball with President Obama.
> I could try to hang out with a rock star.
> I could ask the KKK to change its credo to be pro-diversity.
> I could ask the members of the notorious Westboro Baptist Church to say something nice about other people and the world.

Then I turned this list into an online poll, asking others which one they thought I should try. The vast majority voted for interviewing President Obama, the most famous man in the Western world.

So I made a plan of attack. The thought was to try to generate a firestorm of social media buzz that would somehow get me on Obama's radar. I'd use Twitter, create a YouTube video that would go viral, and start a petition and get thousands to sign it.

Ultimately, I did none of those things. The truth was that hanging out with famous people meant nothing to me. I'd already been on national TV. I'd met some of my favorite authors and business heroes. Plus, I didn't want to put all that effort into what essentially would boil down to a PR stunt. My followers were putting a lot of pressure on me to "go big." But I had to resist the urge to seek their approval.

So I quickly ended my Obama campaign and started something new. I wanted to put my hundredth attempt toward solving a real-world problem, one that regular people face every day, something that could really change someone's life.

And I wanted that someone to be my wife. Ever since I'd quit my job to become an entrepreneur, Tracy had been my rock. Without her, I probably would have folded before I even started my rejection blog. In fact, I might not even have started it at all without her support. I went to bed every night thanking God that I married such an amazing woman.

And I knew that she had professional dreams of her own. Using my "rejection proof" skills to help her fulfill those dreams, just like she helped me to fulfill mine, felt like the perfect way to end my 100 Days.

So one night I asked her: "If you could work for any company in the world, what would it be?" She didn't even have to think about it. "Google!" she said.

Helping Tracy get into Google? Now that's a cause I could go all out for. I loved the idea because:

One, it would be extremely hard. With its theme-park-style office buildings, free gourmet food, on-site massages, volleyball courts, and other legendary perks, Google goes out of its way to create a great environment for its employees. *Fortune* magazine consistently ranks Google as the number one place to work in America. But because it's so desirable, millions of people apply for a Google job every year, and it is notoriously tough to become one of the chosen few. In fact, Google's acceptance rate is below 0.5 percent, more than ten times lower than that of Harvard. To get in, Tracy would need to beat out at least two hundred other applicants.

Two, there are few things in life that people associate more with rejection than a job search. If I could use the principles I'd learned to help Tracy "rejection proof" her way into Google, it could be the ultimate rejection attempt.

Three, Tracy needed it badly. Although she had been rated as a star performer and was highly respected by her colleagues, her company was in an industrywide decline. Many of her coworkers had been laid off, including her boss and some of her closest friends. It's tough to keep your spirits up when working in a struggling environment. You never know what's going to happen next. Tracy needed a career change.

And so there it was, my final challenge. I would go all out coaching and guiding Tracy into a job at Google. We dubbed the project "Finding Google," after the Pixar animation film *Finding Nemo*.

It was a scary proposition, because just like building a company, getting into Google couldn't be done in a half measure. To fully embrace the project, Tracy would need to embrace the risk as well. We decided she should quit her current job and focus 100 percent on the new job search. It would be time-consuming, risky, but fun. Financially and emotionally, we gave ourselves six months to get her a job at Google—the same amount of time she'd given me to launch my start-up.

A job search is a big project, full of ups and downs, rejections and acceptances. So we started by listing the things she could control, including networking, improving her résumé, applying for jobs, and preparing for interviews. Then we listed the things she couldn't control, such as getting an answer from a networking request, securing an interview, having people like her in the interview, and getting a job offer. We vowed to adhere to the core of the rejection-proof principle to detach ourselves from the results while going all out with our effort.

Every day, Tracy would relentlessly focus on her controllable tasks. She sent out dozens of requests to current and former Google employees for phone conversations. They included people in her school network, her former colleagues, and complete strangers. She was always very up front with her intention—asking them to help her find a job at Google. She quickly learned, like I had learned, that it's amazing how nice and helpful people can be if you are honest and just ask. Almost half her requests turned into phone conversations.

During those conversations, Tracy made sure to stay 100 percent authentic to who she was, instead of trying to act a certain way to make people like her. Some people loved her and expressed their desire to help, while others didn't. Tracy tried not to be fazed by phone conversations that went badly or e-mails that were never returned. She focused on the task at hand—and on being herself.

Soon, she started receiving interview requests from Google recruiters, mainly due to referrals from the Googlers Tracy talked to on the phone. There were phone screens first by the recruiters, then by hiring managers, and then by the hiring managers' colleagues. Tracy prepared hard for these interviews, and we would practice over and over again on how to remain calm and be the best she could be. Still, she kept losing out. In one month, Tracy was turned down for three different positions, all for different reasons. Google doesn't give out specific feedback after interview rejections. In one case, Tracy was pretty sure that someone hadn't liked the way she answered a few of the interview questions. In another case, someone didn't think she had the right experience for the job.

Rejection is hard on anyone's emotions, so at first I saw my main job as making sure Tracy would not be negatively affected by it. I urged her to explore every ounce of rejection's upside. "Never waste any rejection," I told her. She could use each rejection as feedback, as a learning tool, and as motivation to keep on trying.

Tracy got it, and she quickly became a rejection-proof expert herself. When the second and third rejections came in, I was more affected than Tracy, and she was the one keeping my spirits up. In fact, I felt so protective of her that I was enraged by some of the reasons. What do they mean she didn't answer the question precisely? Why did they interview her in the first place if she didn't have the experience?

"Calm down," Tracy would say with her soft voice, the same voice she used when putting our son, Brian, to sleep. "Rejection is just an opinion, remember? It reflects them more than me, right?" I agreed. *Wow*, I thought. *Who's the coach now?*

Then, finally, a fourth interview came. This time, the job description fit perfectly with her experience, and she had a fantastic phone interview. Google flew her to their headquarters in Mountain View, California, for an on-site interview. There, she faced a whole team of Googlers, all well prepared with their questions, asking her about every bit of her experience and skills. She came back from the trip exhausted and told me that she really didn't know if she'd done well or not, because she'd had a hard time reading cues from her interviewers, who gave nothing away.

I asked her, "Were you on time?" She said yes.

"Did you answer every question to the best of your ability?" She said yes.

"Were you yourself and not pretending to be someone else?" She answered yes again.

"Then there is nothing to worry about," I assured her. "You did well on everything that you could control. And that's a win!"

One week later, Tracy received an e-mail from the recruiter. We opened it together. Its content and structure were all too familiar. "Thank you for interviewing with us. Unfortunately we decided on another direction. . . ."

Another rejection.

"Well, at least it was fast this time," Tracy said, forcing a smile. By now, she'd sent out hundreds of conversation requests, had countless phone conversations, and four formal interviews. She'd focused on everything she could control and let everything she couldn't control fall as it may. But so far, what she couldn't control had all resulted in rejection.

I tried to hide my disappointment. "Let's take a break," I suggested. "You worked too hard for this. We need to have some fun, too. We need to keep celebrating rejections." So that night, we went out on a date, the first one we'd had since Tracy quit her job. We toasted to rejection, over and over. Deep down, though, I was hurting, because I wanted it so badly for Tracy. It's tough to be rejection proof when it's not you getting rejected, but your loved one.

Two days later, Tracy and I headed to the library, where she would resume her job search project. Along the way I stopped at Starbucks to get her a coffee. On my way back to the car, I saw her talking on the phone. She had a smile on her face that could melt the coldest snow in the world. She hung up just as I opened the door.

She looked at me, with an even bigger smile and with tears in her eyes. "Google changed their mind. They just offered me a job!"

I don't remember what I said afterward, but I do remember hugging her for a long, long time. I remember the pride I felt for this woman. I remember the tears of joy on my face.

Rejection, indeed, is just an opinion. It is so feeble it can even change. It also has a number. In Tracy's case, that number was four, although it felt to us both like four hundred.

I later had a chance to talk with the Google recruiter who had ultimately found Tracy her job. He first corrected me about the size of her competition. In fact, thousands of people applied for the job, not hundreds. But something about Tracy had stuck with him. "Tracy had accomplished a lot in her former job, but was very down to earth and humble," he explained. "She also asked for my advice and trusted me. That meant a lot to me personally as a recruiter."

As for the initial rejection, here's what he said: "Everyone liked her during the interview. For some reason, the team didn't go forward with it. I was so affected by it myself. I remember writing the e-mail and feeling terrible. . . . But the thing was, she took it so well. I've never seen anyone who could take it so positively—never. She even said, 'Please keep me in mind if there are other positions that would fit me.' It made me realize how much she wanted Google, even after all these rejections. That broke my heart . . . and I wanted to advocate for her."

A short time later, the recruiter went back to the team, asking if they had found anyone for the job. They hadn't. So he proposed that they reconsider Tracy. "They said they had interviewed tons of people by then, but still also couldn't get Tracy out of their mind," he said. "Eventually, they decided to reverse course and offer Tracy the position. . . . With my years of experience of being a recruiter, I've never seen that happen. . . . The moral of the story was, treat everyone nicely, even when they say no."

Looking back, getting into Google was very hard, but not impossible. After all, Google has tens of thousands of employees, and they all got in somehow. Moreover, Tracy was an accomplished professional in her own right. There was a chance she would have landed a Google job anyway by herself and through her own job search methods.

Maybe trying to meet Obama or partying with a rock star would have been a more spectacular way to end my 100 Days of Rejection. But I would not have traded this experience for anything else. I got to use everything I learned to help an amazing woman fulfill her dream. For me, there is no bigger prize than that.

## LESSON

1. Detachment from Results: By focusing on controllable factors such as our efforts and actions, and by detaching ourselves from uncontrollable outcomes such as acceptance and rejection, we can achieve greater success in the long run.

CHAPTER 13

# LIVING A NEW MISSION

**L**OOKING BACK TO MY 100 DAYS OF REJECTION, I NOW see it as a journey of transformation. I conquered my fear, gained knowledge and wisdom, and found a new kind of freedom and power. It also led me to a new lifestyle.

Two months after Tracy found her dream job at Google, we moved from Austin to Silicon Valley. Tracy started her new job. She comes home every day energized by the amazing technologies she gets to see and build at work.

As for me, I got to drop off and pick up Brian from daycare, and to write this book—telling our story and sharing what I've learned. All the while, I have continued to make more rejection attempts. I might be going about my normal day when all of a sudden I might ask a stranger if I can retie his shoes, or ask for someone's Twitter account on the street, or ask if someone would dive in a swimming pool with me. I wanted to continue to expand my comfort zone, and to never lose the skill of dealing with rejection that I've developed.

Contrary to popular belief, courage—the ability to do something that's frightening, such as asking for what you need or want, or do the right thing amid rejection and disapproval—is not born but gained. It's like a muscle. You need to keep exercising it to keep it strong. Otherwise, it might weaken or even atrophy. So I use rejection attempts to continue to exercise my courage muscle, stay mentally strong, and keep my confidence flowing.

And I can't help but feel that, in doing so, I've found something that I lost long ago. Remember the kid from Beijing who read Thomas Edison's biography, idolized Bill Gates, and wrote that letter to his family, vowing to buy Microsoft by age twenty-five? The one who walked through that fresh snowfield, dreaming of possibilities?

That kid is back. Actually, he never left. He was simply covered up by layers and layers of fear. But by embracing and overcoming what I was afraid of the most, I have found my new life mission. I am devoting all my entrepreneurial energy to build tools to help as many people as possible. That will require drawing more blueprints, getting more opinions, hiring more people, asking for more investments, and, yes, getting more rejections. However, the difference this time is that I am no longer afraid. Instead, I am intrigued and excited. I want to know, by fighting through my own rejections and helping others to overcome their own, how many more dreams would be fulfilled, how many more cool ideas would be realized, and how many more love stories would be written if we weren't afraid of rejection. More than wondering, I want to help the world—help *you*—make those things happen. If we can all become more rejection proof, wouldn't the world become a much better place?

The rejection-proof world is a wonderful place to live. I hope that this book draws many more people into it—including you. And if you know other people with big dreams and goals who are being held back by fear, please share this book with them. It will help.

If it doesn't help, just buy them a box of donuts. That always helps.

# APPENDIX

# THE REJECTION TOOLBOX

**RETHINKING REJECTION**

1. Rejection Is Human: Rejection is a human interaction with two sides. It often says more about the rejector than the rejectee, and should never be used as the universal truth and sole judgment of merit.

2. Rejection Is an Opinion: Rejection is an opinion of the rejector. It is heavily influenced by historical context, cultural differences, and psychological factors. There is no universal rejection or acceptance.

3. Rejection Has a Number: Every rejection has a number. If the rejectee goes through enough rejections, a no could turn into a yes.

## TAKING A NO

1. Ask "Why" Before Good-bye: Sustain the conversation after the initial rejection. The magic word is "why," which can often reveal the underlying reason for the rejection and present the rejectee with the opportunity to overcome the issue.

2. Retreat, Don't Run: By not giving up after the initial rejection, and instead retreating to a lesser request, one has a much higher chance of landing a yes.

3. Collaborate, Don't Contend: Never argue with the rejector. Instead, try to collaborate with the person to make the request happen.

4. Switch Up, Don't Give Up: Before deciding to quit or not to quit, step back and make the request to a different person, in a different environment, or under a different circumstance.

## POSITIONING FOR YES

1. Give My "Why": By explaining the reason behind the request, one has a higher chance to be accepted.

2. Start with "I": Starting the request with the word "I" can give the requestor more authentic control of the request. Never pretend to think in the other person's interests without genuinely knowing them.

3. Acknowledge Doubts: By admitting obvious and possible objections in your request before the other person, one can increase the trust level between the two parties.

4. Target the Audience: By choosing a more receptive audience, one can enhance the chance of being accepted.

## GIVING A NO

1. Patience and Respect: Rejection is usually a hard message. Delivering the message with the right attitude can go a long way to soften the blow. Never belittle the rejectee.

2. Be Direct: When giving a rejection, present the reason after the rejection. Avoid long and convoluted set-up and reasoning.

3. Offer Alternatives: By offering alternatives to get a yes, or even simple concessions, one can make the other person a fan even in rejection.

## FINDING UPSIDE

1. Motivation: Rejection can be used as one of the strongest motivations to fuel someone's fire for achievement.

2. Self-Improvement: By taking the motion out of rejection, one can use it as an effective way to improve an idea or product.

3. Worthiness: Sometimes, it is good to be rejected, especially if public opinion is heavily influenced by group and conventional thinking, and if the idea is radically creative.

4. Character Building: By seeking rejection in tough

environments, one can build up the mental toughness to take on greater goals.

## FINDING MEANING

1. Find Empathy: All rejections are shared by many people in the world. One can use rejection and suffering to obtain empathy and understanding of other people.

2. Find Value: Repeated rejections can serve as the measuring stick for one's resolve and belief. Some of the greatest triumphant stories come only after gut-wrenching rejections.

3. Find Mission: Sometimes the most brutal rejections in life signal a new beginning and mission for the rejectee.

## FINDING FREEDOM

1. Freedom to Ask: We often deprive ourselves of the freedom to ask for what we want in fear of rejection and judgment. But amazing things often happen only after we take the first step.

2. Freedom to Accept Yourself: Our inner needs of approval-seeking force us to constantly look for acceptance from other people. Yet the people from whom we need acceptance the most is ourselves.

**FINDING POWER**

Detachment from Results: By focusing on controllable factors such as our effort and actions, and by detaching ourselves from uncontrollable outcomes such as acceptance and rejection, we can achieve greater success in the long run.

# ACKNOWLEDGMENTS

My wife, Tracy Xia, is my rock, best friend, and superstar teammate. Her courage and unwavering support have made my entrepreneurial dream, rejection journey, and this book possible.

I gave my talk at the 2013 World Domination Summit. My plan was to launch a Kickstarter campaign to self-publish my book after the talk. Two people in the audience approached me afterward and urged me to consider the traditional publishing route. And I did.

One person was David Fugate. He became my literary agent and a resourceful advisor throughout the process. I've found my own version of Jerry Maguire.

The other person was Rick Horgan, an extraordinary and top-notch editor who eventually acquired my book. Although he couldn't finish the project, I am grateful for his valuable advice in the first half of writing *Rejection Proof*.

I am also extremely fortunate to have Leah Miller to help me finish the project. Her insight and advice gave me much-needed assurance and helped to make *Rejection Proof* a complete book.

One of my best decisions was to hire Jenny Johnston as my personal developmental editor. She was a great partner in the day-to-day editing and structuring of *Rejection Proof*. This book would be nowhere near where it is without her.

Nazli Yuzak, my dear friend and former colleague, gave me tremendous support with the launch of 100 Days of Rejection. She will forever be my Turkish cousin.

Heath and Alyssa Padsett, the twenty-three-year-old Austin couple, took my advice and turned their honeymoon into a crazy fifty-state RV trip. Now they are helping me with my book launch. It's crazy how the universe works sometimes. I am very grateful to know these two.

I also want to thank Bill Gates for his original inspiration. His own story planted the entrepreneurial seed in my young mind and grew to where it is today.

Last, Jackie Braun, the donut maker at Krispy Kreme, is a real heroine. Without her kindness and amazing customer service, there would be no Olympic donuts and *Rejection Proof*.